THE SCOTTISH REGIMENTS

Diana M. Henderson

SECOND EDITION

D0094268

HarperCollins*Publishers*

HarperCollins Publishers
PO Box, Glasgow G4 0NB

First Published 1993
Second Edition 1996

© Diana M. Henderson 1993, 1996

ISBN 0 00 471025 8

Reprint 9 8 7 6 5 4 3 2 1 0

A catalogue record for this book is available from the British Library

Illustration Acknowledgments

All illustrations contained in this book have been supplied by the
respective regimental museums and headquarters, except where
specified below; those supplied by The Highlanders appear by permission
of the regimental Trustees.

All tartans, regimental badges, maps and illustrations on pp 31, 48, 55, 81
(top), 103 (right), 116, and 151 (right) (© HarperCollins)

pp 33, 37, 89, 123, 153, 159 (Author's collection)

pp 46, 57 (© Mike Moore, taken from *Desert War*, Mike Moore, London,
1991. Reproduced by permission of Penguin Books Ltd.)

pp 29, 91, 92 (Scottish United Services Museum)

pp 30 (Imperial War Museum)

pp 96, 97 (Lt Col. Helen Homewood, RLC)

Printed in Italy by Amadeus S.p.A.

Contents

The Regiments

Appendices

The fighting capability of the Scots has been recognised throughout British history. Formed into trained and disciplined regiments in government service from the late seventeenth century and employed in all parts of the world to gain and defend the Empire, they acquired an enviable reputation for their dedication and loyalty. In the twentieth century they have fought in two world wars and in many lesser conflicts and made a significant contribution to the good name of the British Army wherever it has been deployed.

The regimental system is peculiar to the British Army, and nowhere has it a firmer base than among the people and clans of Scotland. The tradition of family service, where son follows father into the local regiment, is firmly ingrained in the Scottish culture and creates that special sense of family and continuity that is so typical of Scottish regiments. It is for this reason that the amalgamations between so many Scottish regiments in the run-down of the Army since the end of the second world war has caused so much distress throughout Scotland.

Dr. Henderson has written a lively and interesting history of each of the regiments from their earliest days and traced their descent through various amalgamations to the present day. I have no doubt that it will become a reference book for serious students and scholars of military history, but there is also much to interest the general reader.

Introduction

Over the past three centuries, the Scottish soldier has established a fiercesome reputation for his fighting ability, a reputation which in modern times has been consistently proven and reinforced by his feats of arms in theatres of conflict throughout the world. The history of the Scottish regiments is not therefore just any story; it is a story of courage, of comradeship and of dogged perseverance.

In the past, many Scottish regiments were formed in time of war and disbanded thereafter, as was the old way, or alternatively, they were subsequently amalgamated, renumbered and renamed. Thus the regiments which survive today reflect the current stage (but not the endpoint) of an evolutionary process and represent in themselves only a small part of a combined record of service stretching back over hundreds of years. The British regimental system has carefully preserved, recorded and maintained the individual historical components of each of these surviving regiments and despite the amalgamations and inevitable merging of identities, an extraordinary pride is still taken in the old battle honours, in regimental traditions and in individual and distinctive items of uniform.

To those who have never had personal experience of it, this regimental pride, loyalty and spirit is sometimes difficult to understand, particularly as it is often just as strong amongst the mothers, fathers, wives and children of members of the regiments as amongst the soldiers themselves. This is due in no small part to the fact that, because many of Scotland's regiments are based in and associated with particular areas of the country, they tend to be family affairs, with sons following fathers and grandfathers into the local regiment, in which perhaps a brother or an uncle is also serving.

For many years, Scotland has provided a high proportion of soldiers for the British Army. In spite of the developments of modern warfare which emphasise standardisation, Scottish regiments have succeeded in retaining their own distinctive character, most obviously expressed in their modes of dress and music. The Highland regiments are, in fact, now the only troops in Europe to wear national dress as an everyday military uniform.

However, for many people, the bagpipes, the tartan and the glengarries can seem outmoded and contrived, and it is not difficult to find evidence to support this belief. For example, historically, the use of the highland bagpipe is not strictly correct in the context of the Lowland regiments who originally used a specifically lowland form of the instrument. The ubiquitous glengarry was only introduced in the 1840s when Lt Col. The Hon. Lauderdale Maule of the 79th Cameron Highlanders adapted the old 'humle' bonnet from which the present cap is derived. In addition, it was as late as 1881 before tartan was adopted by the the Lowland regiments, at a time when the 'Highland' image and the cloth itself had become widely popular throughout Scotland.

Historically inaccurate, outmoded and contrived as the image of the Scottish soldier may appear, the professionalism and the individual regimental pride, traditions and loyalty are very real and it is this reality which, in truth, binds men together in dangerous circumstances and in times of extreme stress. Thus, in this book I have attempted to describe briefly the proud history of Scotland's cavalry, guards and infantry regiments by providing not simply the basic facts and figures, but by also highlighting their particular traditions and the role of individual soldiers, all of whose contributions serve to make Scotland's regiments so unique. Finally, in this the second edition, I have to record with particular feeling the amalgamation of the Queen's Own Highlanders and The Gordon Highlanders; one Highland regiment less is nobody's gain.

Acknowledgments

Writing this book has been great fun but I cannot honestly say that it has been easy; it has been produced in the face of enormous changes in the organisation of the British Army, particularly with regard to certain Scottish regiments, the sudden death of a close friend and collaborator on the project, and the extraordinary pressures of a full-time job.

However, the task of producing the text was made easier by the unstinting help and generosity extended to me by a wide range of individuals. The co-operation and advice of the regimental secretaries and those working in the regimental headquarters and museums has been absolutely invaluable and I should like to add a special thanks to all of the serving soldiers who patiently gave up their time to be photographed in the various orders of dress; the staff of the Infantry Depot, Glencorse and the recruiting staff of The Scots Guards, The King's Own Scottish Borderers and The Royal Highland Fusiliers were especially helpful in this respect.

Thanks also go to Major Campbell Graham (Rtd), Scots Guards of the Royal British Legion Scotland; to Lieutenant Colonel Helen Homewood RLC (TA) who lent me papers and photographs regarding her uncle, John Erskine VC; and to Victoria Bruce and Karen Hooker who typed the text and may well have learnt some Scottish military history into the bargain! James Carney of HarperCollins has been tremendous, pressurising, cajoling, encouraging and simply bullying me into producing the complete text with endless energy and enthusiasm; he has worked hard on this volume and I appreciate greatly what he has done.

To my great sadness, my long-standing friend and the much-admired Scottish military historian, William Boag, died during the time of writing the first edition. He was working on reviewing the text, much of which was subjected to his detailed and knowledgeable scrutiny. I will always be grateful to him for almost twenty years of friendship, humour and encouragement.

Diana M. Henderson
1996

Dedicated to the soldiers of Scotland

The Royal Scots Dragoon Guards

Carabiniers and Greys

The Royal Scots Dragoon Guards is Scotland's most senior regiment and the only regular army regiment of cavalry north of the border. This famous unit, whose history is punctuated with the great cavalry battles of three centuries, was formed in 1971 from The Royal Scots Greys (2nd Dragoons), the 3rd or Prince of Wales's Regiment of Dragoon Guards and the Carabiniers (6th Dragoon Guards). In 1922, the two latter regiments had been amalgamated to form The 3rd Carabiniers (Prince of Wales's Dragoon Guards) which in turn was amalgamated with The Royal Scots Greys .

It is still common in Scotland today for The Royal Scots Dragoon Guards to be referred to affectionately as 'the Greys'. This in no way belittles the distinguished history of the 3rd Carabiniers but calls to mind the famous and beautiful grey horses of The Royal Scots Greys. The regiment, which is now mechanized and part of the Royal Armoured Corps, recruits throughout Scotland and has its home base in the Castle at Edinburgh.

The Royal Scots Dragoon Guards achieved world renown when their combined regimental band and pipes and drums recorded *Amazing Grace* which made it to number one on the hit parade.

Badge

The badge of The Royal Scots Dragoon Guards is an eagle in silver upon a plaque, 'Waterloo', surmounting crossed carbines in gilt, with the scroll 'Royal Scots Dragoon Guards'.

As in all amalgamated regiments, the badge and uniform of the Royal Scots Dragoon Guards is a subtle blend and weave of the history and traditions each of its components. The eagle, for example, commemorates the capture of the Imperial eagle and standard from the French 45th Regiment at the Battle of Waterloo in 1815 by The Royal Scots Greys.

During the morning of the battle, the Greys were positioned behind the centre of the British line. In front, were Belgians and Sir Thomas Picton's Division, including the Royal Scots, the 42nd Black Watch, the 79th Cameron Highlanders and the 92nd Gordon Highlanders. The Belgians fell back as the infantry came under fire, leaving the whole of the British centre dangerously exposed, including the Highlanders. In the confusion, the noise and the thick powdered smoke

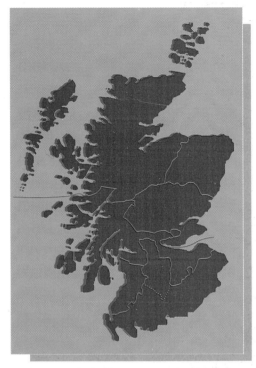

Regimental Recruiting Area

which enveloped the scene, the famous Union Brigade, comprising the Royal Dragoons, The Royal Scots Greys and the Inniskilling Dragoons (representing the three countries of the United Kingdom), were ordered to charge.

The power and momentum generated by charging massed cavalry was chilling. Forcing their way through one French column, sheer dynamism carried the Greys through to a second. In a vicious fight, the French 45th Regiment courageously defended their eagle and standard which proudly bore their great battle honours of 'Austerlitz', 'Jena', 'Friedland', 'Essling' and 'Wagram' - honours which had earned them the title 'The Invincibles'. After a fierce hand-to-hand fight, Sergeant Ewart of the Greys, managed to carry off the French eagle and standard, which he bore away in triumph.

Two hundred men and 224 horses of the Greys were killed or wounded in the battle. Later, Napoleon was to refer to the regiment as 'les terribles chevaux gris' (those terrible grey horses). Ewart received a commission from the Prince Regent. In 1936, his body was removed from a disused graveyard in Manchester and reintered on the esplanade of Edinburgh Castle. On Waterloo Day 1956, the French eagle, which had lain in the Royal Hospital, Chelsea, was formally returned to the regiment. It was carried at the head of The Royal Scots Greys up the Royal Mile to Edinburgh Castle, where it was handed over for safekeeping in front of Ewart's tomb.

The charge of the Royal Scots Greys at Waterloo, 1815

The eagle in the badge and the honour 'Waterloo' are of tremendous significance to The Royal Scots Dragoon Guards as, indeed, are the crossed carbines. A carbine or 'carabin' is a light musket formerly issued to some regiments of horse. As the title 'fusilier' came to be considered an élite in the infantry, so did the title 'carabinier' when applied to regiments of horse. It was for their distinguished service with King William's army at the Battle of the Boyne in 1690, that the distinction and special title of 'The King's Carabiniers' was conferred upon the 9th Regiment of Horse in 1691. The 9th Horse are one of the three constituent ancestor regiments of the Royal Scots Dragoon Guards.

The Royal Scots Dragoon Guards have three mottos: *Nemo me impune lacessit* (no one provokes me with impunity); *Ich dien* (I serve), which is the motto of the Prince of Wales and inherited through the 3rd Dragoon Guards; and 'Second to none', the motto of The Royal Scots Greys. This latter motto is a play on words emphasizing that, although the regiment takes second place amongst the regiments of the cavalry of the line, they are still the oldest of them all.

Regimental Origin

The Royal Scots Dragoon Guards has its origins in three entirely distinct regiments. Firstly, there was the Royal Regiment of Scots Dragoons, initially raised in Scotland in 1678 as three independent troops of dragoons to quell the activities of the Covenanters and formed as a regiment in 1681. Mounted on grey horses, this regiment acquired the nickname and later the official title of The Royal Scots Greys. Secondly, there was the 4th Regiment of Horse raised in the English counties of Worcestershire, Oxfordshire, Northamptonshire, Bedfordshire, Huntingdonshire and Middlesex as a result of the Duke of Monmouth's rebellion in 1685. Thirdly, the 9th Regiment of Horse was also raised at the time of Monmouth's Rebellion. The men of the 9th Regiment of Horse were raised in Hampshire, Nottinghamshire, Hertfordshire, Yorkshire and Suffolk. The successors of these two latter regiments, the 4th and the 9th, were amalgamated in 1922 as a result of the reorganisation of the cavalry after the First World War and assumed the new title of the 3rd Carabiniers.

In 1971, the 3rd Carabiniers were amalgamated with The Royal Scots Greys to become The Royal Scots Dragoon Guards. While the 3rd Carabiniers had origins very firmly south of the border, in the amalgamation , it was the Scottish partner, The Royal Scots Greys, who became dominant. Very few of the traditions of the 3rd Carabiniers survive except, for example, the Princes of Wales's feathers worn as an arm badge, the yellow facings and the yellow colour of the 'Vandyke' braid of the hat bands.

Each of the three elements of The Royal Scots Dragoon Guards has, however, a distinguished history and fighting reputation. The Royal Scots Greys served in actions against the Covenanters at the Battle of Bothwell Brig (1679), against the

Earl of Argyll in Monmouth's Rebellion, and against Viscount Dundee, 'Bonnie Dundee', in 1689. In 1694, the regiment joined King William's army in the Netherlands where they took part in the siege and capture of Namur. In 1702, they returned to the Netherlands under the Duke of Marlborough where they were engaged at Schellenberg Hill and Blenheim (1704), Ramillies (1706), Oudenarde (1708) and Malplaquet (1709).

Back in Scotland, the Greys were in action against the Jacobites in 1715 at Sheriffmuir. Four years later, in an extraordinary incident, 500 predominantly Spanish troops were landed on the west coast of Scotland at Kintail in support of the another Jacobite uprising (the '19). These foreign troops were joined by 1500 Highland men. As they advanced through Glenshiel, the Greys cut off the pass and the rebels were routed by supporting infantry.

The regiment served in the Netherlands again during the War of the Austrian Succession (1740-48), and in Germany during the Seven Years' War (1756-63). The Greys then spent a long period in Britain before joining the Duke of York's disastrous expedition to the Low Countries in 1793. For 20 years thereafter, the Greys remained on home duty. Then, in 1815, the regiment took part in the historic action at Waterloo.

In 1854, they were sent to the Crimea and, along with the 6th Inniskilling Dragoon Guards, conducted the famous charge of the Heavy Brigade at the Battle of Balaklava. The Greys were in action during the South African War (1899-1902) and served in both a mounted and dismounted role in the First World War. In 1920, they were sent to Palestine and, two years later, to India. In March 1941, the Greys, the last surviving horsed British cavalry, were mechanized and M3 Stuart and M3 Grant tanks were issued to them. The regiment was present at key Second World War actions such as El Alamein (1942), the Normandy landings (1944), and the advance into Germany (1944-45).

The other components of The Royal Scots Dragoon Guards had equally distinguished histories. The 4th Horse and the 9th Horse, like the Greys, took part in the Netherlands campaign of 1694 and also returned there in 1702 under the command of the Duke of Marlborough. All three regiments earned the battle honour 'Blenheim'. After a long break, during which the 9th served mainly in Ireland, the 4th, 9th and the Greys were together again in Germany during the Seven Years' War (1756-63) fighting the French.

It was during this war that the cavalry under George, Lord Sackville were conspicuous in their failure to charge the beleaguered enemy at the Battle of Minden in 1759. One year later, at Warburg, 22 squadrons of British cavalry, including the 4th, the 9th and the Greys, under the Marquis of Granby, conducted a brilliant charge, routing the French and forcing them to abandon their guns. It was during this charge that the marquis, who personally led his troops into battle, lost his wig. His distinguished, but bald, head could be clearly seen by all around him and the incident is believed to be the origin of the expression 'going for them bald-headed'.

The Royal Scots Greys at Glenshiel during the Jacobite rebellion of 1719

The 4th and the 9th underwent several changes of both name and number, but by 1788 they were styled the 3rd or Prince of Wales's Regiment of Dragoon Guards and the 6th Dragoon Guards (the Carabiniers) respectively. It was under these titles that the 3rd fought during the Duke of York's campaign in Flanders in 1794 and the 6th served in the ill-fated expedition to seize Spanish treasure in the Argentine in 1807.

The 3rd then fought for five hard years in the Peninsular campaign at Talavera (1809), Albuera (1811) and Vittoria (1813). In 1868, the regiment landed on the Red Sea coast of Africa to march over 400 miles in an extraordinary expedition to overthrow the truculent Emperor of Abyssinia. Twenty years later, they were part of the Nile expedition to rescue General Gordon in Khartoum. Meanwhile, the 6th were engaged in the Crimea, the Indian Mutiny and Afghanistan (1879-80). They then joined the Greys in South Africa during the Boer War of 1899-1902.

After continuous service during the First World War, the 3rd and the 6th were amalgamated in 1922 to become the 3rd Carabiniers, affectionately known simply as 'the Carabiniers'. While the changing needs of modern warfare meant that it was not logical to retain horses, it was certainly not easy for the regiment to part with them; however, in 1938, mechanization was decreed for the Carabiniers in India.

During the Second War World (1939-45), the regiment fought with both deter-

The Royal Scots Dragoon Guards in the Gulf, 1991

mination and distinction in the campaign in Burma from Imphal to Rangoon with General Slim's 14th Army. In 1961, the Carabiniers, in perhaps a foretaste of things to come, were rushed to the Sultanate of Kuwait in order to prevent a threatened Iraqi invasion.

United with The Royal Scots Greys in 1971 under the title of The Royal Scots Dragoon Guards, the regiment served again in Kuwait during the Gulf War (1991). During the war, one of their young officers, Second Lieutenant Richard Telfer, won the Military Cross.

Second Lieutenant Telfer had joined the regiment only four months before the Gulf War. As one of the most junior officers in the regiment, he commanded a troop of three Challenger tanks ordered to advance with infantry into Iraqi territory against a series of enemy positions. Leading his troop and the supporting infantry into the centre of one emplacement, he sighted the enemy and moved forward alone in the darkness, opening fire with his machine gun, thereby drawing the enemy fire and providing both covering fire and an indication of the enemy position. At the same time and with great courage, he described all that he could see and directed the assaulting infantry to precisely the correct position. Telfer's Military Cross was one of several awards to the regiment in the Gulf, which included a Military Medal awarded to Corporal Kenneth Anderson.

The regiment on parade 1991

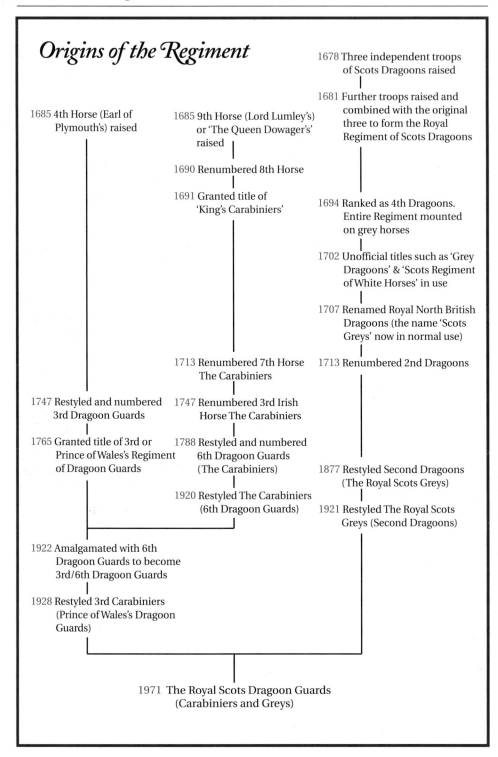

Origins of the Regiment

1678 Three independent troops of Scots Dragoons raised

1681 Further troops raised and combined with the original three to form the Royal Regiment of Scots Dragoons

1685 4th Horse (Earl of Plymouth's) raised

1685 9th Horse (Lord Lumley's) or 'The Queen Dowager's' raised

1690 Renumbered 8th Horse

1691 Granted title of 'King's Carabiniers'

1694 Ranked as 4th Dragoons. Entire Regiment mounted on grey horses

1702 Unofficial titles such as 'Grey Dragoons' & 'Scots Regiment of White Horses' in use

1707 Renamed Royal North British Dragoons (the name 'Scots Greys' now in normal use)

1713 Renumbered 7th Horse The Carabiniers

1713 Renumbered 2nd Dragoons

1747 Restyled and numbered 3rd Dragoon Guards

1747 Renumbered 3rd Irish Horse The Carabiniers

1765 Granted title of 3rd or Prince of Wales's Regiment of Dragoon Guards

1788 Restyled and numbered 6th Dragoon Guards (The Carabiniers)

1877 Restyled Second Dragoons (The Royal Scots Greys)

1920 Restyled The Carabiniers (6th Dragoon Guards)

1921 Restyled The Royal Scots Greys (Second Dragoons)

1922 Amalgamated with 6th Dragoon Guards to become 3rd/6th Dragoon Guards

1928 Restyled 3rd Carabiniers (Prince of Wales's Dragoon Guards)

1971 The Royal Scots Dragoon Guards (Carabiniers and Greys)

Tartans

The only men of The Royal Scots Dragoon Guards to wear tartan are the pipers. The tradition originates from The Royal Scots Greys in 1946 when a number of pipers came to the regiment from demobilised Scottish Territorial Armoured Corps Units. These pipers were granted permission by George VI to wear the Royal Stewart tartan. The Greys then had officially recognized pipes and drums. The first man of the regiment to attend the much sought-after Pipe Major's Course at the Army School of Piping in Edinburgh was Piper Major Halley in 1959.

Royal Stewart tartan

Clan or Scottish Family Affiliations

The Greys were raised by General Thomas Dalyell of The Binns, West Lothian. Here, indeed, was an extraordinarily able and accomplished man. The product of an ancient Scottish family, Dalyell was a dedicated soldier and anti-Covenanter. He was a captain in the Earl of Morton's Regiment at the siege of La Rochelle (1628) and then served with ruthless efficiency as a colonel commanding Scottish troops during the Irish Rebellion (1641). An ardent royalist, he was captured by the Cromwellian army at the Battle of Worcester (1650) and imprisoned in the Tower of London, until he escaped in May 1652. Armed with letters of recommendation, he made his way to Russia, where he was appointed a general in the Russian army and fought against the Poles and Turks.

In 1665, Dalyell was recalled to Scotland by Charles II and he took command of a small force to suppress the Covenanters who were opposed, amongst other things, to episcopacy in Scotland. The Covenanters advanced from the west towards

Edinburgh and Dalyell engaged the rebels and routed them after a stiff fight on the steep slopes of the Pentland Hills at Rullion Green in the evening light of 28th November 1666. In 1667, Dalyell relinquished command only to be recalled again as Commander-in-Chief, Scotland, from 1679 until his death in 1685, aged 86. It was during this latter period of his life that he raised the additional troops of horse which were formed into a regiment known as The Royal Regiment of Scots Dragoons.

The Carabiniers have no clan or Scottish family affiliations as they originated from English regiments.

Battle Honours

The battle honours of The Royal Scots Dragoon Guards tell the story of three distinguished regiments and their role in the service of their country.

'Waterloo', the great battle honour of the Greys, is matched only by that awarded for their courage at the Battle of Balaklava. Early on the morning of 25th October 1854, few allied troops were to be found in the vicinity of the key supply port of Balaklava in the Russian Crimea. The main part of the army had departed to lay siege to Sevastopol when the Russians attacked the outlying pickets, which were manned by the Turks. Advancing towards the town, the Russian cavalry engaged the 93rd Highlanders and were repulsed, but they were supported by a further large body of cavalry, who continued to advance under the cover of a ridge of hills.

The Heavy Brigade of British cavalry, under the command of General Sir James Scarlett and including the Royal Scots Greys and the 6th Inniskilling Dragoons, advanced onto the field of battle. They began to approach at right angles to the

Russians, still unaware of the position of the advancing Russian cavalry reinforcements, screened by the ridge. Suddenly, the tips of the Russian lances were spotted and the Greys and the Inniskillings wheeled to their left and set about dressing their line. The Russians appeared over the ridge and halted to watch the Greys below them in the valley, calmly dressing their lines as if on parade. There were 3000 Russian horsemen and less than 600 British. The Greys' officers continued to dress their ranks with their backs to the enemy. Scarlett sat quietly in front of them, waiting until everything was ready and ignoring Lord Lucan, who impatiently ordered them to advance.

Only when all the details had been attended to, was the order to charge given. The trumpet sounded and Scarlett galloped forward and disappeared into the mass of Russian troops. The Royal Scots Greys followed him with the Enniskillens charging in hot pursuit. A densely-packed, chaotic, slogging battle ensued. There was neither the time nor the space for parade ground sword drill movements; the Greys cut, hacked and slashed their way through, turned and hurtled headlong back into the fray. After only five minutes, the Russians were visibly wavering. The remaining British cavalry squadrons now charged. A few minutes later, the Russians were in

The Regimental Standard

14

The charge of the Royal Scots Greys at Balaklava, 1854

retreat. Exhausted and blood-stained, and with tears running down their cheeks, the Greys watched their enemy disappear over the horizon. They had executed one of the most daring cavalry against cavalry charges in history.

The heroic actions of the 3rd Carabiniers in Burma (1944) served to sustain and reinforce this bold cavalry tradition. In March 1944, the Japanese 15th Division under Yamauchi advanced to encircle the 17th Indian Division at Imphal. The British Forces in Imphal, including the 3rd Carabiniers, withdrew into a series of defensive 'boxes' to form a perimeter, but so successful was the Japanese advance that many of these positions could only be supplied from the air. Eight miles north-east of Imphal, the Japanese captured the key position of Nunshigum Ridge, which they immediately reinforced with a series of complex and deep defensive bunkers.

Recapturing this dominant position was of vital importance and the task was allocated to the 3rd Battalion of the 9th Jat Regiment of the Indian Army, with B Squadron of the 3rd Carabiniers in support. The attack began on 11th April, but the bunkers were so deep, the ridge so precipitous, and the defenders so determined that the assault had to be abandoned. Air attack and artillery made no impression against these bunkers and two days later, the ground attack was renewed, this time, by the 1st (Prince of Wales's Own) Dogra Regiment, closely supported by the Carabiniers' tanks.

With great difficulty, the tanks negotiated the near-impossible terrain. The attackers were extremely exposed and because of the steepness of the hillsides, the tank commanders had to guide their drivers from open turrets. As they reached the summit, the supporting air strikes and artillery barrage lifted and the Japanese emerged from their bunkers shooting the tank commanders at close range. The Carabiniers squadron leader and all of the officers were killed. All of the Dogra officers became casualties. The attack was in grave danger of faltering when squadron Sergeant

The Heavy Brigade in action

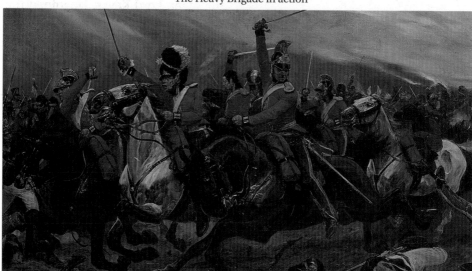

Major Craddock and Subadar Ranbir Singh took command and ordered a flanking movement, drawing the enemy fire and enabling the infantry to capture the hilltop. Sergeant Major Craddock was awarded the Distinguished Conduct Medal and Subadar Singh the Indian Order of Merit.

Each year on Nunshigum Day (13th April), B Squadron of The Royal Scots Dragoon Guards celebrate this great battle honour by parading under the command of their squadron Sergeant Major and without their officers.

Victoria Cross Winners

Sgt H. Ramage	2nd Dragoons (Royal Scots Greys)	1854	Crimea
Sgt J. Grieve	2nd Dragoons (Royal Scots Greys)	1854	Crimea
Lt Col. G. Keyes, M.C.	Royal Scots Greys	1941	North Africa

Lt Col. G. Keyes V.C. M.C.

The Royal Scots Dragoon Guards have three Victoria Cross winners. Two of the medals were gained during the Crimean War. The third was awarded to Lieutenant-Colonel Geoffrey Charles Tasker Keyes of The Royal Scots Greys and 11th (Scottish) Commando as a result of one of the most interesting and unusual attacks of the Second World War.

Keyes was born in Aberdour, Fife, on 18th May 1917, the son of Admiral of the Fleet, Lord Keyes. He joined the Greys in 1937 and, after volunteering for commando services, raised a troop of 11th (Scottish) Commando in 1940. Keyes had been awarded the Military Cross as a result of actions in Syria in 1941.

On the eve of 'Operation Crusader', the code name for General Sir Claude Auckinleck's advance on Tobruk in November 1941, Keyes set out on a dramatic mission. The plan was to land six officers and 53 men from submarines and to proceed inland through the desert. They had four objectives: to attack the Italian headquarters; to attack the Italian intelligence centre; to attack the German headquarters; to attack General Rommel's personal villa to the west of Beda Littoria near Tobruk. Accompanying the party was

Colonel Robert Laycock, the original commander of the Special Service Brigade.

The landings and the attacks had all been rehearsed. However, on the night of the 13th-14th November, when the assault landing took place, there was a strong gale blowing. As a result, it took some seven hours instead of the planned ninety minutes to get the first 28 men ashore. When the second submarine made its approach, it grounded temporarily and in the gale and high seas, seven boats and eleven men were swept overboard. The submarine immediately withdrew, taking with her some of the men and vital weapons and equipment. Several men were lost at sea.

In the morning, the remainder met at the rendezvous point. They were wet, cold and without some all-important equipment. Laycock now decided that the objectives were too ambitious for the numbers available and limited the mission to attacks on the Italian and the German headquarters. The idea of the assault on Rommel's personal villa was abandoned, as was the planned assault on the Italian intelligence centre.

By the night of 16th November, under Keyes' leadership, the men reached a cave five miles from the German headquarters. The cold was intense and the rain never-ending. On the evening of the 17th, Keyes returned from a reconnaissance, divided the group into two and briefed each party as to their mission. Keyes himself led the attack on the German headquarters.

At the edge of the perimeter, one of the party tripped noisily and two sentries were alerted. Keyes' second-in-command, Captain Robin Campbell, promptly shouted at them in fluent German and they went away. Once through the perimeter, only one sentry remained and he was silently killed by Keyes. The group identified the headquarters building and Campbell banged on the door shouting in German until the occupants opened up. As the door opened, Keyes pushed the soldier back with his revolver but the startled German shouted a warning and chaos broke loose as a fire-fight began in the hall. Keyes then kicked open one of the doors leading from the hall and emptied the contents of his revolver into the occupants of the room. He rushed into a second room where the occupants were the first to fire. A single shot rang out, Keyes was thrown back and he was dead within a few moments.

Dragging Keyes' body outside, Campbell began the withdrawal. In the darkness and confusion, the covering party mistook him for a German and let loose a burst of machine gun fire. Seriously wounded, Campbell could no longer continue and Sergeant Terry assumed command. He attempted to blow up the building, but the fuses, soaked through by the rain, were useless. They sabotaged the main generator with a grenade and withdrew. The following night, the survivors from both parties, now only 22 in number, met on the beach and signalled to the submarine offshore. For some reason, the signalling failed to bring the boats to pick them up. As dawn broke, the party hid in a wadi where they were attacked by some Arabs and then a group of Italians. Laycock had no option but to order the men to split into small groups and make their own way to the Allied lines as best they could. Only Laycock and Sergeant Terry made it through. The rest were captured. Keyes, aged 24, was buried with full military honours by Rommel's chaplain, with the general in attendance. Keyes was posthumously awarded the Victoria Cross.

Against a background of extraordinary courage and gallant determination, the mission remains one of the most unusual episodes of the war in North Africa. The original object seems to have been to attack both headquarters and to assassinate Rommel. Commando raids were still in their infancy and there seems to have been serious shortfalls in intelligence, planning, co-ordination and communications. In fact, Rommel had moved his headquarters sometime before and was nowhere near the site of the raid that night. Nothing, however, can detract from the undoubted bravery of those who took part.

The charge of the 3rd Dragoon Guards at Honnechy, 1918

Regimental Music

Regimental Band

March past in quick time	*3rd Dragoon Guards*
March past in slow time	*The Garb of Old Gaul*

Regimental Band and the Pipes and Drums

To play the Regiment off Parade	*Scotland the Brave*
	The Black Bear

Mounted Marches

Walk	*Men of Harlech*
Trot	*The Keel Row*
Canter	*Bonnie Dundee*

Pipe Marches

March past in quick time	*Highland Laddie*
March past in slow time	*My Home*

One of the most outstanding features of the regimental music of The Royal Scots Dragoon Guards is the black drum horse, which carries the kettle drums and the white bearskin of the kettle drummer. The white bearskin is now unique in the British army and when the drum horse is not on parade, the white bearskin is worn by the bass drummer. The black drum horse called Ramillies stands in stark contrast to the traditional grey horses of the regiment. Both Ramillies and his predecessor, Trojan, were presented to the regiment by Her Majesty Queen Elizabeth II.

At the Amalgamation Parade of The Royal Scots Greys and the 3rd Carabiniers in 1971, the Band Master of The Royal Scots Greys and the Pipe Major collaborated to make a musical arrangement for band and pipes of the old Scottish hymn Amazing Grace. As the Queen inspected the Greys for the last time, a solo piper began and the pipes and drums and the regimental band took up the melody. The arrangement was to bring the newly-formed The Royal Scots Dragoon Guards to world-wide notice, with five weeks at the top of the British popular music charts. The rendition also became number one in Canada, South Africa, Australia and New Zealand, and reached number seven in the USA. This haunting and evocative melody is still enormously popular, although few are aware of its origins and its links with the emotional moments of the final inspection of The Royal Scots Greys.

Allied and Affiliated Regiments

Canada

The Windsor Regiment (RCAC)

Australia

The 12th/16th Hunter River Lancers (RAAC)

New Zealand

1st and 2nd Squadrons, New Zealand and Scottish (RNZAC)

South Africa

The Natal Carabiniers

(Top) Drum Horse 'Ramillies' presented to the Regiment by H.M. The Queen
(Bottom) H.M. The Queen meets the Band Master, the Band Sergeant Major,
the Pipe Major and the Drum Major

The Scots Guards

T he Scots Guards – even the title of this famous regiment conjures up a picture of high standards, immaculate turn-out, determination, fighting quality and loyal service. Once a Guardsman, always a Guardsman; Scots Guardsmen world-wide are intensely and rightly proud of their regiment's history which dates back to 1642. It is a history which includes battle honours from the siege of Namur in 1695 to the Falklands War of 1982.

Today, the regiment recruits throughout Scotland, exacting the same traditionally high standards of entry, although The Scots Guards are seldom seen north of the border. Both battalions take their turn in royal duties on the Queen's Guard at Buckingham Palace and at St. James's Palace, at Windsor and at the Tower of London.

In 1991, it was announced that the 2nd Battalion Scots Guards was to be placed in 'suspended animation', moving from Edinburgh to Windsor in late 1993 to be merged with the 1st Battalion

Badge

The badge of The Scots Guards is the Star of the Order of the Thistle, being the Cross of Saint Andrew, with rays in the angles, the thistle in the centre circle is surrounded by the words *Nemo me impune lacessit* (No one provokes me with impunity).

The Most Ancient and Most Noble Order of the Thistle was founded in 1687 and revived by Queen Anne in 1703. The Order is restricted to 16 distinguished Scots, thus making it more exclusive than the Order of the Garter and perhaps the rarest honour in Europe. In 1962, King Olav of Norway was the first foreigner to be admitted to the Order in over 200 years.

The Scots Guards first began to use the Star of the Order of the Thistle as a badge around the time of the union of the Parliaments of England and Scotland in 1707. However, the saltire or Saint Andrew's cross, the thistle and the motto were appearing on colours presented to The Scots Guards companies as early as 1662.

Regimental Origin

In 1642, England was on the verge of civil war and Ireland was in a state of rebellion against the Scottish and Protestant settlers who had colonised the six counties of Ulster. Determined to put down this rebellion, Charles I authorised Archibald, 1st Marquis of

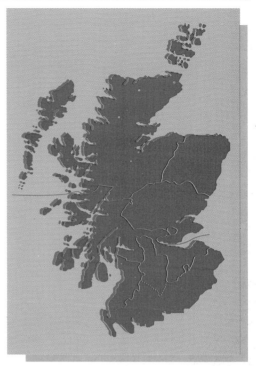

Regimental Recruiting Area

Argyll to raise a regiment to act as his Royal Guard for the campaign. As it turned out, the king did not personally lead his army in Ireland, but Argyll's Regiment, from which The Scots Guards finds its origin, served there for seven long years, returning to Scotland in 1649 so depleted in numbers that they were merged with nine other regiments raised at the time and called 'The Irish Companies'.

In 1649, Charles I was executed and in 1650, the Irish Companies welcomed back his son, Charles II from his exile in France. At Falkland Palace in Fife, the Irish Companies were renamed the King's 'Lyfe Guard of Foot'. Under this title, The Scots Guards unsuccessfully fought with the Royal Army against Cromwell at both Dunbar (1650) and Worcester (1651). After this latter battle, the Scots army ceased to exist.

When Charles II was restored to his throne in 1660, companies of Scottish Foot Guards were reraised in 1662 to garrison Edinburgh, Dumbarton and Stirling castles. Expanding first to six and then to thirteen companies by 1666, George, Earl of Linlithgow was appointed as their colonel and the regiment fought against the Covenanters at Rullion Green (1666) and at Bothwell Brig (1679).

In 1688, true to its Protestant principles, the regiment, then known as the Scotch or Scots Guards, declared their allegiance to William of Orange and fought in Marlborough's Wars in the Low Countries at Walcourt (1691), Steenkirk (1692), Landen (1693) and the siege of Namur (1695).

Scots Guards saving the colours at the Battle of Alma, 1854

It was in 1704 that a Highland Company was raised 'for the security of the Highlands and the adjacent country against threats and depredations'. These men wore Highland dress and carried Highland weapons and were disbanded after ten years service in 1714.

In 1712, Queen Anne changed the name of the regiment to The 3rd Regiment of Foot Guards. During the War of the Austrian Succession, the 3rd Foot Guards fought at Dettingen (1743) and Fontenoy (1745) and during the Seven Years' War at the capture of Cherbourg (1758). When the British colonies in America declared independence in 1776, a composite detachment of guards, including the 3rd Foot Guards, fought at the battles of Brandy Wine Creek (1777) and Guildford Courthouse (1781), returning to England after the surrender at Yorktown in 1781, when the British garrison, including the Guards, capitulated to the Americans. They marched from their stronghold with colours cased and drums beating a tune entitled *The World Turned Upside Down*.

From 1789 to 1815, the 3rd Guards played an outstanding role in the French Revolutionary and Napoleonic Wars, culminating in the 2nd Battalion's heroic defence of the farm of Hougoumont on the field of Waterloo, fighting alongside The Coldstream Guards and the 1st Guards (Grenadiers).

In 1831, the 3rd Guards regained their Scottish title and became Scots Fusilier Guards and the whole regiment was clothed in bearskin caps. During the Crimean War, the regiment fought at the Alma, Inkerman and at Sevastopol (1854). In 1877,

Members of the regiment on the ramparts of Edinburgh Castle

Origins of the Regiment

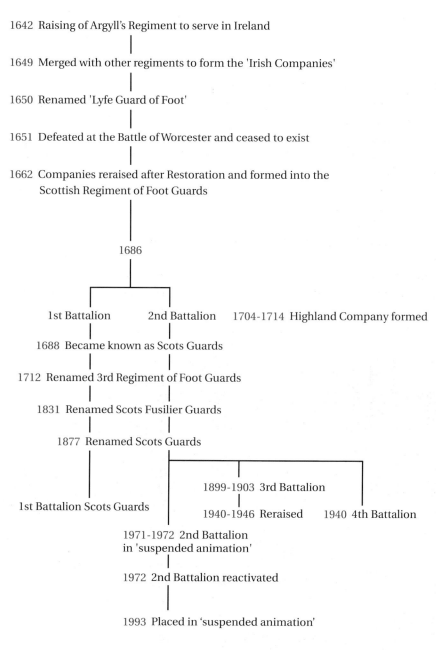

1642 Raising of Argyll's Regiment to serve in Ireland

1649 Merged with other regiments to form the 'Irish Companies'

1650 Renamed 'Lyfe Guard of Foot'

1651 Defeated at the Battle of Worcester and ceased to exist

1662 Companies reraised after Restoration and formed into the
Scottish Regiment of Foot Guards

1686

1st Battalion   2nd Battalion   1704-1714 Highland Company formed

1688 Became known as Scots Guards

1712 Renamed 3rd Regiment of Foot Guards

1831 Renamed Scots Fusilier Guards

1877 Renamed Scots Guards

1899-1903 3rd Battalion

1st Battalion Scots Guards   1940-1946 Reraised   1940 4th Battalion

1971-1972 2nd Battalion
in 'suspended animation'

1972 2nd Battalion reactivated

1993 Placed in 'suspended animation'

Sentry duty at Edinburgh Castle, 1951

Men of the Scots Guards after hearing the news of the Argentine surrender, The Falklands, 1982

Queen Victoria restored the title 'Scots Guards' to the regiment. Under Sir Garnet Wolseley, the 1st Battalion Scots Guards fought at the Battle of Tel-el-Kebir in Egypt (1882) and after distinguished service in South Africa in the Second Boer War (1899-1902), The Scots Guards played their full part in the great battles of the First World War including the retreat from Mons, Marne, Aisne, Ypres, Loos, Somme, Cambrai and the Hindenberg Line. Between the wars, duty for the Scots Guards included Hong Kong, Singapore, Egypt and Palestine.

During the Second World War, the 1st Battalion Scots Guards fought in Norway, North Africa and Italy including the landings at Anzio in 1944. The 2nd Battalion served in the Western Desert, Italy and North West Europe, while the 3rd Battalion, which was now armed with Churchill tanks, also served in North West Europe from the Normandy landings to the final victory in Germany.

After the War, the 2nd Battalion formed the British Guard of Honour at the Potsdam Conference, while the distinguished 3rd Battalion, which had been both the first through the Siegfried Line and to cross the Rhine were disbanded in 1946.

During the 'peace' that followed the Second World War, The Scots Guards served in Malaya, Cyprus, Egypt, Kenya, Indonesia and Northern Ireland. In March 1971 the 2nd Battalion was placed in 'suspended animation' but was reformed in Edinburgh in January 1972. It was this battalion which sailed on the *Queen Elizabeth II* to land at San Carlos, East Falkland to fight and finally to capture Mount Tumbledown.

Scots Guards uniforms, 1992

Tartans

The tartan worn by the pipers of The Scots Guards is the Royal Stewart, with trews, plaids, pipe ribbons and garter flashes of the same tartan. The officers wear a small Royal Stewart tartan patch on each side of their khaki Service Dress Cap. A small tartan patch is also worn behind the Cap Star on berets.

Royal Stewart tartan

Clan or Scottish Family Affiliations

The Scots Guards in their original formation as royal guards were raised and commanded by the Marquis of Argyll and can thus claim links with the powerful Clan Campbell.

After the Restoration of the monarchy in 1660, the Foot Guards were reraised and were commanded by George Livingston, 3rd Earl of Linlithgow. George Livingston was born in 1616 and, as an ardent royalist, he had suffered severely under Cromwell's Protectorate. In 1662, he was made a Privy Councillor. He was a descendant of Sir James Livingston of Callendar who was created Lord Livingston in 1458. George Livingston was present at the Battle of Rullion Green (1666) against the Covenanters and was acting Commander-in-Chief in Scotland between 1667 and 1674, during which time he was said to have exercised a 'firm and beneficial rule in the disaffected West'. The title of Earl of Livingston was attainded in 1716 because James, the 5th Earl, supported the Jacobites in the rising of 1715.

Scots Guards uniforms, 1971

Battle Honours

It is difficult in the case of The Scots Guards, whose battle honours stretch over almost 300 years, to select any one for particular attention. The names of Dettingen, Salamanca, Inkerman, Tel-el-Kebir, Gheluvelt and Anzio all conjure up the determination and bravery epitomizing the regiment.

Many regiments of the British army have as one of their battle honours 'Waterloo'. For The Scots Guards, however, one word — 'Hougoumont' — sums up this great battle. The chateau of Hougoumont was one of the key points on the battlefield at Waterloo. A complex of buildings which included a chapel, barns and a walled garden, Hugoumont covered an area of some 500 square yards. Outside the surrounding walls were orchards.

On the evening of 17th June 1815, the Duke of Wellington, in command of the allied armies, ordered the Light Companies of the Guards Brigades, including the 3rd Guards (Scots Guards) to occupy the chateau complex as the key position on the right of the allied line. This was accom-

The Regimental Colour

plished unopposed, while the remainder of the Guards brigades took up position behind the farm. That night, the men at the chateau set to work fortifying the buildings, loop-holing the walls and barricading all the gates, except the north one, which was left open, so that ammunition and reinforcements could be brought in.

The French attacks began at 11 o'clock on the morning of 18th June. The first attack failed, but a second soon developed and the defenders came under siege from three sides. The guardsmen, including those of the 3rd Guards, who were now outside the walls had to fight their way back through the north gate. Before the gates could be shut and barricaded, however, the French rushed the entrance and forced their way in. Coldstream Guardsmen and men of the 3rd Guards fought desperately in a hand-to-hand struggle to keep the French out and to close the heavy doors. Finally, with dead and wounded littering the courtyard entrance, the gates were closed. Along with the Coldstreamers, Sergeants Fraser, Brice, McGregor, and Alston and Private Lister, all of the 3rd Guards, are recorded amongst those who closed the gates

Within the walls of Hougoumont, 2000 men now faced an enemy of 30,000. Attack and counter-attack followed without mercy throughout the early afternoon as the Guards fought through the orchard of the chateau and defended their position with accurate and devastating fire from the walls. However, the buildings were set alight and many of the wounded in the barns burnt to death. Finally, two battalions of the king's German Legion counter-attacked outside Hougoumont and the chateau was relieved.

Almost one-third of Napoleon's infantry had been utilized to capture Hougoumont. The vain attempt has cost 8000 French lives. The attacks had been continuous and 400 men of the 3rd Guards were casualties in the battle. Hougoumont was a battle within a battle and the closing of the gates was a critical factor in Wellington's success at Waterloo.

In April 1982, 167 years later, the 2nd Battalion The Scots Guards prepared for the recapture of the Falkland Islands after the Argentinian invasion. The Scots Guards were to play a distinguished part in this most unusual campaign. They trained in Wales and then embarked for war on the liner *Queen Elizabeth II*. The battalion first landed at San Carlos and then moved up to be landed off HMS *Intrepid* at Bluff Cove, fifteen miles from the Falkland's capital, Port Stanley. It was the middle of a cold, blustery, wet South Atlantic winter. On 13th June, the battalion moved to their assembly area below Mount Harriet. Thirty men of Headquarters Company The Scots Guards began a diversionary attack under Major Hon. Richard Bethell. At 8.30 p.m., one of the armoured vehicles operating in support of this group struck a mine. The remaining vehicles halted and The Scots Guards moved forward to a cluster of enemy sangers. These seemed to be abandoned, but suddenly firing started and the whole position exploded into life. The men of Headquarter Company then began a two-hour battle fighting their way through 11 enemy trenches, one by one, with grenades and small arms.

Meanwhile, at 9.00 p.m. the main attack was launched. As the Scots Guardsmen approached the main objective of Tumbledown Mountain, they met fierce enemy machine-gun fire. The whole mountain position was heavily defended by very determined Argentinian troops and the rough broken terrain, the darkness, the flurries of snow and the strength of the enemy position all added to the difficulties.

Throughout the night the fierce fighting continued. At 2.30 a.m. Major John Kiszeley, commanding Left Flank Company, led a charge on the crest of the mountain and at 6.00 a.m., Right Flank Company began the third phase of the battalion's attack. It took, however, a further six hours of sustained and determined attacks with phosphorus grenades and automatic weapons to clear the enemy from their bunkers.

In this battle, The Scots Guards lost 9 men killed and 43 men wounded. Tumbledown was perhaps the most strongly defended Argentinian position on the island for which the defenders fought with stubborn determination. The capture of the mountain by the 2nd Battalion The Scots Guards signalled the prelude to the Argentinian surrender in Port Stanley on 14th June 1982.

Victoria Cross Winners

Brevet Major R. J. Loyd–Lindsay	Scots Guards	1854	Crimea War
Sgt J. Knox	2nd Bn. Rifle Brigade Scots Guards	1854	Crimea War
Sgt J. McKechnie	Scots Guards	1854	Crimea War
Private W. Reynolds	Scots Guards	1854	Crimea War
Ensign J. Craig	Scots Guards	1855	Crimea War
Private J. Mackenzie	2nd Bn Scots Guards	1914	France
2nd Lt G. A. Boyd-Rochfort	Special Reserve, 1st Bn Scots Guards	1915	France
L/Sgt F. McNess	1st Bn Scots Guards	1916	France
Sgt J. MacAulay, D.C.M.	1st Bn Scots Guards	1917	France
L/Sgt H. Blanshard Wood, M.M.	2nd Bn Scots Guards	1918	France
Lt The Lord Lyell	1st Bn Scots Guards	1943	North Africa

The Scots Guards can lay claim to eleven Victoria Cross winners from the Crimean War to the North African battlefields of the Second World War. Exemplifying the courage of all of these Scots Guardsmen is Lance-Sergeant Fred McNess. Fred McNess was born in 1892 in Bramley, Leeds although his father came from Perth

L/Sgt F. McNess V.C.

and had served in the Royal Engineers. Fred was a carter's assistant before the First World War and he enlisted in the 3rd (Reserve) Battalion The Scots Guards on 30th January 1915. By August 1916, he had been promoted to Lance-Sergeant. On the morning of 15th September 1916, the 1st Battalion The Scots Guards, with whom Fred McNess was now serving, were in the line at Ginchy near Albert in France and were poised for an attack north-eastwards towards Lesboeufs. At 6.20 a.m. the creeping artillery barrage began and the guards moved forward behind it at 30 yards distance. Lance-Sergeant McNess and his party of men reached the first German trench, found a path through the wire and then began to move along the communication trench. By this time, the advancing Guardsmen were already under heavy fire from the flank where the Germans still held positions. Many men had already been wounded or killed. The Germans recovered quickly and, in their turn, began working down their own trench, bombing and firing as they went.

For an hour and a half, Sergeant McNess with a corporal and a small party of men counter-attacked with such grim determination that, slowly but surely, the Germans were driven back and a 'block' was established. When their own bombs ran out, they used captured enemy material. In the course of the fighting, a bomb exploded in McNess' face, blowing away the left side of his neck, part of his jaw and his teeth. Notwithstanding, he fought on until exhausted by loss of blood. By his own account, he then walked two miles to a field dressing station and from there was carried three miles by German prisoners to an ambulance. He was invalided to London where he underwent major surgery to reconstruct his jaw.

On 9th of December 1916 he was driven from hospital to Buckingham Palace to receive his Victoria Cross. Pale and weak, he spoke with the king quietly and privately for some time. He was the only Victoria Cross holder to be presented on that day. Sergeant McNess did not finally leave hospital until July 1918. He returned to Leeds and worked for some time in the Leeds City Engineer Department. He continued to suffer from severe headaches and depression as a result of his wounds and tragically, in 1956, shortly after his retirement, he took his own life.

Regimental Music (Pipes and Drums and Regimental Band)

March past in quick time   Heilan' Laddie

March past in slow time   The Garb of Old Gaul

Advance in Review Order Scotland the Brave

Company Marches

1st Battalion

Right Flank	Greenwood Side
B Company	The Drunken Piper
C Company	The Back of Benachie
Left Flank	Scotland the Brave
Headquarter Company	Black Bear

Uniforms of the Regimental Bands, 1971

The pipers of The Scots Guards were formally authorised after 1856, although pipers had played with the battalions for many years previously, serving soldiers being drawn from the ranks for the purpose. The first Pipe Major was Ewan Henderson.

The early pipers of The Scots Guards, however, did not enjoy the kudos of their Highland regimental counterparts. Indeed, so anglicized did the Guards become that pipers were discontinued between 1868 and 1870 at the request of the officers. From then on, piping flourished in the Guards, primarily led by the great Pipe Major Willie Ross, who served for 22 years with the regiment. From 1905 to 1917, he was Pipe Major of the 2nd Battalion.

Pipe Major Ross was a most remarkable player and composer. He wrote fine tunes, which are still played both in recital and competition. These include *Captain Norman Orr-Ewing, Leaving Port Askaig* and *John Morrison, Esq of Assynt House.*

In 1919, Pipe Major Willie Ross was appointed to succeed Pipe Major John MacDonald to run the Army Class of the Piobaireachd Society, later to become the Army School of Piping. With humour, charisma and in some cases a kindly, but firm hand, Willie Ross held the appointment of Instructor of the Army Class until 1958, teaching hundreds of army pipers. He is widely considered to be one of the most influential figures in 20th-century piping.

This tradition of excellence has been continued in The Scots Guards by influential prize-winning players such as Pipe Major Angus MacDonald M.B.E. and Sergeant Brian Donaldson.

Regimental Toast

Deoch slainte na ban Righ (Here's a health to the Queen)

Allied and Affiliated Regiments

Australia

3rd Battalion The Royal Australian Regiment

The Royal Scots

The Royal Regiment

The Royal Scots, the 1st Regiment of Foot and holders of the coveted position at the right of the line, are the oldest surviving regiment in the British army and the senior regiment of infantry. It was formed in 1633 by John Hepburn, who was authorised to recruit in Scotland in order to add to a body of men who were survivors from much earlier regiments. These earlier regiments are so old that their origins are obscure and so The Royal Scots lay claim to an ancestry of considerable antiquity. It is not for nothing that the regiment is nicknamed 'Pontius Pilate's Bodyguard'. Today, the regiment recruits in Edinburgh, the Lothians, and Tweedale with the regimental headquarters situated at Edinburgh Castle. In 1991, it was announced that The Royal Scots were to amalgamate with The King's Own Scottish Borderers; however, early in 1993, this move was abandoned following a re-assessment of future force requirements.

With their long, continuous and distinguished history, The Royal Scots have a style all of their own. Over a number of years, they have established a great reputation for piping, and two of their most famous pipe majors are Alex Matheson, who served with the 1st and 3rd Battalions between 1889 and 1913, and G. S. Allan, who served with the 1st Battalion from 1907 to 1919 and with the 2nd Battalion from 1921 to 1930.

Badge

The badge of The Royal Scots is the Star of the Order of the Thistle. In the centre, St Andrew and his cross, worn on a red cloth background.

Regimental Motto

Nemo me impune lacessit (No one provokes me with impunity).

Regimental Origin

In 1633, John Hepburn of Athelstaneford was commissioned by Charles I and the Scottish Privy Council to raise recruits in Scotland, based on a nucleus of men who had served in various other ancient and historic regiments. It was agreed between Louis XIII of France and Charles I that this regiment was to enter French service. This arrangement was not unique: it was common during this period for regiments to be raised in Scotland for service in continental armies. Ancestors of Hepburn's regiment are believed to include the Scots Archer Guard in France; the Green, or Scots Brigade,

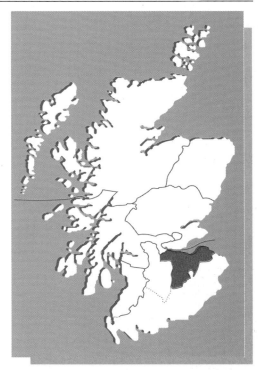

Regimental Recruiting Area

which fought heroically for King Gustavus Adolphus of Sweden; and Gray's Regiment in the service of the King of Bohemia, in which regiment, Hepburn himself was a captain.

Hepburn was killed in 1636, and was succeeded briefly by his brother George, and then by Lord James Douglas. The regiment temporarily came home in 1662 and in 1667, but it was not until 1678 that it was finally recalled and were put onto the Irish establishment. As Dumbarton's Regiment (Lord George Douglas, Earl of Dumbarton was Colonel from 1653 to 1688), it fought with distinction in the defence of Tangier in North Africa, from 1680 to 1684. At the Battle of Sedgemoor which ended the Monmouth Rebellion in 1685, the regiment established its precedence and fought this battle in the coveted position on the right of the line.

During the Glorious Revolution of 1688, the regiment remained loyal to King James II. It was only after the departure of the Catholic Earl of Dumbarton and the purging of many of the officers and men, that the regiment finally gave its allegiance to the Protestant successors, William and Mary of Orange. For the remainder of the 17th century, The Royal Scots served in Holland during the War of the League of Augsburg and were present at the siege of Mons, Steenkirk (1692), Landen (1693) and at the siege and capture of Namur (1695).

2nd Battalion The Royal Scots, 1688

Grenadiers, 1703

Under the Duke of Marlborough, The Royal Scots fought against the French in the War of the Spanish Succession (1701-14), where they gained for themselves an enviable reputation in the actions at Schellenberg, Blenheim, Ramillies, Oudenard, Malplaquet and Venloo, amongst others. In 1713, they returned to serve on detached duties in Ireland, essentially policing and keeping order. After a disastrous expedition to Jamaica, where hundreds of men died of disease, the regiment again fought the French during the War of the Austrian Succession (1740-48) and were present at the Battle of Fontenoy (1745). The 2nd Battalion The Royal Scots fought in Scotland in 1746 against Prince Charles Edward Stuart's army both at Falkirk and Culloden.

In 1751, numbers were assigned to the colours of regiments, and The Royal Scots were designated as the 1st or The Royal Regiment of Foot. Amongst the unusual duties which followed were service in North America against the French colonists, and in South Carolina against the native Indians. Some companies were sent to the Caribbean and other companies served to remove the French from St John's in Newfoundland. In 1799, the 2nd Battalion took part in a raid on Ostend and also gained the battle honour 'Egmont-Op-Zee'. The same battalion served under Sir Ralph Abercromby at Aboukir Bay, at Alexandria and at Cairo against the French in 1801. In 1807, the 2nd Battalion was sent to India. In 1812, the 1st Battalion embarked for Canada, where they fought the Americans in several battles, including the action near Niagara Falls in 1814. The 3rd Battalion was present during the arduous withdrawal to Corunna in the Peninsular War (1809-14) and at Bussaco, Fuentes de Oñoro and at Salamanca, amongst others.

In 1812, the title 'Royal Scots' was officially conferred upon the regiment. A fourth battalion sailed with an expedition to Sweden in 1813. This battalion in 1814 conducted the extraordinary feat of arms of marching from Lübeck in Germany to Holland, where it took part in the siege at Bergen-Op-Zoom.

The following year, the 3rd Battalion The Royal Scots participated in the historic battle of Quatre-Bras and they were also engaged at Waterloo, where they recaptured from the French one of the key positions on the battlefield, the farmhouse of La Haye Sainte.

Following the Napoleonic Wars, the 1st Battalion The Royal Scots served in the West Indies. The 2nd Battalion took part in the Second Mahratta War in India, followed by action in the Burmese War in 1825. In 1854, the 1st Battalion joined the Allied army in the Crimean War (1853-56) and fought at the Alma, at Sevastopol and at the great Battle of Inkerman (1854). In 1860, the 2nd Battalion, which was already in Hong Kong, moved to north China, and during this arduous and difficult campaign it played a key role in the capture of the Taku Forts.

In 1882, the regiment with its two battalions was renamed The Royal Scots (Lothian Regiment). In common with other Lowland regiments, tartan trews of Government, or Black Watch, tartan were adopted. The 1st Battalion was then sent to South Africa during the Second Boer War (1899-1902).

Origins of the Regiment

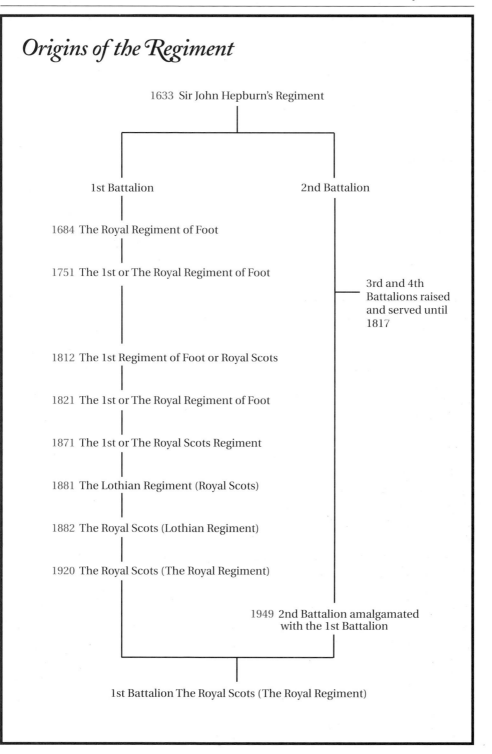

1633 Sir John Hepburn's Regiment

1st Battalion

2nd Battalion

1684 The Royal Regiment of Foot

1751 The 1st or The Royal Regiment of Foot

3rd and 4th Battalions raised and served until 1817

1812 The 1st Regiment of Foot or Royal Scots

1821 The 1st or The Royal Regiment of Foot

1871 The 1st or The Royal Scots Regiment

1881 The Lothian Regiment (Royal Scots)

1882 The Royal Scots (Lothian Regiment)

1920 The Royal Scots (The Royal Regiment)

1949 2nd Battalion amalgamated with the 1st Battalion

1st Battalion The Royal Scots (The Royal Regiment)

With the outbreak of the First World War, the 2nd Battalion was sent to France in August 1914. The Royal Scots took part in major battles from Mons (1914) to Ypres, Loos, the Somme, Arras and Passchendaele (1917) to Gallipoli and Palestine.

With the end of the war on the Western Front in 1918, the 2/10th Battalion The Royal Scots took part in the extraordinary invasion of northern Russia in support of the anti-Bolshevik forces (1918-1919) in which Archangel was occupied and Murmansk seized. The regiments engaged in a series of actions against the Bolsheviks across the flat and frozen tundra. Most of the soldiers involved simply remember marches along apparently never-ending railway lines interrupted by brief and bloody skirmishes. Eventually, the expedition was withdrawn.

Inter-war service included Macedonia, Burma, India, Aden, Ireland and China. In 1939, the 1st Battalion was sent to France to occupy the Maginot line. An exhausting withdrawal included bitter fighting in the village of Le Paradis where The Royal Scots broke up a determined enemy attack and the Germans began shooting the wounded and machine-gunning parties of prisoners. Few of the battalion finally managed to reach Dunkirk to be evacuated. The 2nd Battalion were in Hong Kong, and after a determined and difficult resistance, only about 100 men survived to surrender to the Japanese.

The reconstituted 1st Battalion took a notable part in the battles of Kohima (1944), the relief of Kohima, Aradura Spur and at Mandalay (1945)while the 2nd Battalion was in action in Italy. After landing in Holland in 1944, the romantically styled 'Dandy 9th' — the 7/9th (Highland) Battalion, a Territorial Army battalion of The Royal Scots — fought to clear the Scheldt and the 8th Battalion took part

'Pontius Pilate's Bodyguard' (from a cartoon by E.V. Howell, 1931)

Captain N. Soutar M.C.

in the Normandy landings and the liberation of France, Belgium and Holland.

In 1949, the 1st and 2nd Battalions were amalgamated and subsequently saw active service in Korea, Egypt, Cyprus, Aden and Northern Ireland.

In 1991, The Royal Scots formed part of the Allied army in the Gulf War and it was during the advance on Kuwait City that Captain Norman Soutar, commanding A Company of the 1st Battalion The Royal Scots was awarded the Military Cross. Captain Soutar, leading one of many mounted assaults, chose to advance rapidly under his own artillery barrage in order to ensure complete surprise. Another who distinguished himself in this action was Private Thomas Gow of The Royal Scots. Private Gow had already been in action for 24 hours when his company was held up by a resistance from a dug-in enemy position. Realising that the momentum of the attack was being lost, he ordered his comrades to cover him as he crawled forward. Despite exploding mines and bomblets, he got within 20 metres of the enemy vehicle and destroyed it. He then went on to charge two more bunkers, clearing them with grenades, and capturing several enemy soldiers. He was awarded the Military Medal.

Private T. Gow M.M.

Officer, 1842

Lance Corporal, 1992

Tartans

The Royal Scots did not wear tartan until they adopted Government tartan trews in 1881. In 1907, these were changed to Hunting Stewart tartan.

In 1933, The Royal Scots celebrated their tercentenary and the celebratory parade at Aldershot was attended by King George V. On this colourful occasion, and as the first regiment in the British army to celebrate a tercentenary, the king announced that he desired to identify himself with his oldest regiment. 'It gives me great pleasure,' he said, 'to confer upon your pipers the right to wear my personal tartan – the Royal Stewart. I know that you and your successors will ever hold fast to your high traditions and that Scotland and the Empire may always rely on The Royal Scots'.

One of the most romantic and colourful Territorial Battalions of The Royal Scots was the 9th (Highlanders) Battalion. From the outset, this battalion did not wear trews, but wore the kilt. They were raised as a result of the war in South Africa, recruited from Highland men resident in the City of Edinburgh and were known as 'the Dandy 9th'. These Highland men served with considerable distinction during the First World War at the battles of the Somme, at High Wood and at Beaumont Hamel. The only units which now wear the old Hunting Stewart kilts are the Pipe Band of The City of Edinburgh Universities Officer Training Corps, the Officer Cadets of Tayforth Universities Officer Training Corps and the pupils of Queen Victoria School, Dunblane.

Royal Stewart tartan

Clan and Scottish Family Affiliations

The Royal Scots, throughout their long and distinguished career, have been associated with several of the great houses of Scotland, from John Hepburn of Athelstaneford in East Lothian, who raised the regiment to Lord George Douglas, later the Earl of Dumbarton, who commanded the regiment for over thirty years. Other commanding officers included Lord George Hamilton, who later became the Earl of Orkney.

Battle Honours

The battle honours of the Royal Scots reflect the extraordinary service of this great regiment over a period of more that 350 years.

The most unusual battle honour is probably 'Archangel 1918–1919', when the regiment, after extensive service in the First World War was sent to Russia to fight the Bolsheviks. This expedition, about which so little is known, was undertaken against a background of great trials and hardships at a time

Queen's Colour, 1st Bn The Royal Scots

when Europe was exhausted by war and the old Russian Empire had collapsed.

Another unusual battle honour for The Royal Scots is 'Taku Forts and Peking 1860'. These actions took place during the Second China War. Hostility had been mounting on the Chinese mainland for some considerable time as a result of the European demand to acquire trade access points in the form of duty-free ports. In 1858, the 2nd Battalion The Royal Scots were in Hong Kong, and in 1860, they joined the expedition to north China, primarily to avenge the death of four British diplomats, but also to collect a huge indemnity from the Emperor for his failure to open up the treaty ports. It was intended as a punitive expedition.

It was decided to try to take the ports from the rear, and the landings of a British and French force began on 1st August 1860 near Phtang, some three miles from the main objective. The British contingent was under the command of General Sir Garnet Wolsley. The logistics were difficult, the muddy conditions made marching a nightmare, and there was a considerable amount of looting, particularly by the French.

At day-break on 21st August, the attack on the forts began with an artillery bombardment which hit the powder magazine of the northern-most fort. Undeterred, the Chinese defenders stood their ground, and displayed a courage and coolness which drew admiration from their attackers. Eventually, the British troops, The Royal Scots amongst them, managed to get ladders to the walls. In bitter hand-to-hand fighting, jabbing and slashing with swords and bayonets, the forts were occupied and the Chinese withdrew.

There then followed an advance to Tientsin, during which the Emperor's summer palace was burnt. The armies finally entered Peking on 24th October. For The Royal Scots, this was an extremely arduous and unglamorous campaign, involving great hardships of mud and extreme heat and cold, coupled with a determined and ruthless enemy, and not always the greatest cooperation from the French allies.

Victoria Cross Winners

Private J. Prosser	2nd Bn The Royal Scots	1855	Crimea
Private H. H. Robson	2nd Bn The Royal Scots	1914	Belgium
Private R. Dunsire	13th Bn The Royal Scots	1915	France
Capt. H. Reynolds	12th Bn The Royal Scots	1917	Belgium
Lt D. S. McGregor	6th Bn The Royal Scots	1918	Belgium
Cpl R. E. Elcock	11th Bn The Royal Scots	1918	France
Private H. McIver	2nd Bn The Royal Scots	1918	France

Private H.H. Robson V.C.

Amongst these Victoria Cross winners, it is difficult to pick out one and select him as an example of all the rest, but the case of Henry Howey Robson serves to illustrate the courage exhibited by young men in the face of battle.

Private Henry Howey Robson was born in South Shields, Co Durham on 27th May 1894. At this time, it was not uncommon for north country men to move to join Scottish regiments and Private Robson joined the 2nd Battalion The Royal Scots. At the time, the 2nd Battalion was the 'home' battalion of the regiment and on the outbreak of war, it sailed for France and took up positions in the area of Mons on 23rd August 1914. After the retreat to the Marne, and the critical battles on the Aisne, Henry Robson and his battalion moved through the area of Neuve Chapelle. By December, they were in the area of Kemmel in Belgium near the little town of Wijtschate, nicknamed by the soldiers 'white sheet'. The weather was bitterly cold, the battalion was seriously depleted and the soldiers who had served since August were exhausted.

The German army, despite many attempts, failed to make the critical breakthrough to the sea, but the fighting continued relentlessly. On 14th December 1914, The Royal Scots began an attack on the enemy positions in front of them. The weather was bitterly cold and the enemy fire was heavy and accurate. As the attack developed, a non-commissioned officer in front of Robson was hit and lay wounded. Private Robson left his trench under heavy fire, with complete disregard for his own safety, and rescued the man, bringing him back under cover. He then tried to bring in another comrade, but was himself hit. Despite this, he continued his attempts to rescue the wounded man until he was again struck and could do no more. Henry Robson was only twenty at the time, and displayed the kind of determination that has characterised his regiment throughout the centuries. After the war, Henry Robson emigrated to Canada, where he died on 4th March 1964.

Regimental Pipe Music

Pipe Marches

March in quick time	*Dumbarton's Drums*
March in slow time	*The Garb of Old Gaul*
The Charge	*Monymusk*
March on with the Band	*Scotland the Brave*

Company Marches

A Company	*The Barren Rocks of Aden*
B Company	*Marie's Wedding*
C Company	*The Black Bear*
D Company	*The Liberton Polka*
Headquarter Company	*The Steamboat*

Piping has a strong tradition in The Royal Scots. One of the earliest known illustrations of military pipers is in 'The Destruction of the Mole at Tangier 1684' by the Dutch painter, Stuyp. This clearly shows four pipers, and it is believed that they must have belonged to The Royal Scots, as no other Scots were garrisoned there at the time. In more modern times, several members of the regiment have been placed in the Highland Society of London's Competition and regimental winners of the Gold Medal at Oban have been Pipe Major G. S. Allan and Pipe Major Alex Matheson.

Allied and Affiliated Regiments

Royal Gurkha Rifles

Canada

The Canadian Scottish Regiment (Princess Mary's)
The Royal Newfoundland Regiment

The Royal Highland Fusiliers

Princess Margaret's Own Glasgow & Ayrshire Regiment

The Royal Highland Fusiliers is one of Scotland's proudest and most distinguished regiments. The current title dates from 1959 when The Royal Scots Fusiliers and The Highland Light Infantry were amalgamated to continue their service as a single regiment. More popularly known today simply as the R.H.F., the regiment can trace its origins as far back as 1678 and is Scotland's second oldest surviving regiment.

The battle honours and service of The Royal Highland Fusiliers record the colourful part which the regiment has played in their country's service from Blenheim in 1704 to Kuwait in 1991. Today, the regiment recruits in Glasgow and Ayrshire and its link with Scotland's second great city, made formal in 1923, and with its west coast burghs, gives The Royal Highland Fusiliers its distinctive, proud, friendly, determined, 'no nonsense' characteristics.

Badge

The badge of The Royal Highland Fusiliers is a flaming grenade, bearing the monogram 'HLI', surmounted by a crown. The regiment's motto is '*Nemo nos impune lacessit*' (No one provokes us with impunity).

The grenade with the flaming fuse is taken from the cap-badge of The Royal Scots Fusiliers. It was customary in fusilier regiments to wear the regimental device upon the bowl of the grenade and in the case of The Royal Highland Fusiliers, the letters 'HLI' are worn, representing the other half of the 1959 amalgamation. Great confusion is often caused concerning which of the three letters is superimposed upon the other and the badge is thus often misrepresented. In fact, the 'I' forms the base, then the 'L' and finally the 'H' superimposed on the other two.

The Royal Highland Fusiliers also wear white hackles or plumes in certain forms of head dress. The white hackle was a standard one for grenadiers and fusiliers and was worn by The Royal Scots Fusiliers from 1768 to 1866. It was restored to the regiment in 1902 to mark its distinguished service during the South African War of 1899–1902.

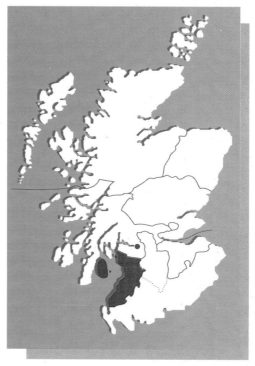

Regimental Recruiting Area

Regimental Origin

The R.H.F. can trace their origins to three outstanding regiments: The Royal Scots Fusiliers raised in 1678 as the Earl of Mar's Regiment and numbered 21st, MacLeod's Highlanders raised in 1777, originally as the 73rd but renumbered the 71st in 1786 and The Highland Regiment raised in 1787 and numbered 74th.

In 1881, the 71st and the 74th regiments were linked and formed the 1st and 2nd Battalions of The Highland Light Infantry. In 1959 the surviving 1st Battalion of The HLI was amalgamated with The Royal Scots Fusiliers to form The Royal Highland Fusiliers. Against the background of these amalgamations and changes of title can be set the distinguished history of each component part.

The Royal Scots Fusiliers were raised by Charles Erskine, 5th Earl of Mar in 1678. At that time, it was customary for a regiment to take the name of its colonel and thus the regiment was entitled The Earl of Mar's Regiment and quickly nicknamed 'The Earl of Mar's Grey Breeks', after the colour of their breeches. The regiment was specifically raised for the purpose of dealing with the threat posed by the rebellious Covenanters from the south west of Scotland.

After the Battle of Bothwell Brig in 1679, The Royal Scots Fusiliers played a part in nearly every major war in the latter 17th, the 18th and the 19th centuries. They

Officer and Corporal, 74th Highlanders, *c.* 1855   Lance Corporal, 1992·

fought at Steenkirk (1692), Landen (1693), Blenheim (1704), Ramillies (1706), Oudenarde (1708) and Malplaquet (1709); against the rebellious Highlanders at Sheriffmuir (1715), at Dettingen (1743) and Fontenoy (1745), and again, against the Highlanders at Culloden (1746). During the American Revolution they were present at Stillwater (1777) and Saratoga (1777) and later at Martinque and Guadaloupe (1794). In 1814, the 21st were in America and after the American defeat at Bladensburg they entered Washington where the regiment ate the Presidential banquet prepared to celebrate a British defeat.

This distinguished early history earned the regiment their 'Royal' prefix by 1712 and for many years they were also known as 'Marlborough's Own'. After the union of the English and Scottish Parliaments in 1707, they were titled The Royal North British Fusiliers.

In the peace that followed Waterloo, the 21st, amongst other duties, was sent to guard convicts in Australia. During the Crimean War the regiment won honours at Inkerman, 'The Soldiers Battle' and at Sevastopol. This was followed by action in the Zulu War of 1879, the 1st Boer War and operations in Burma and on the North West frontier of India.

In 1881, the regiment was restyled The Royal Scots Fusiliers. Eighteen battalions served during the First World War with tremendous distinction in France and Flanders. Most of the same ground was fought over again by the regiment during the Second World War, when they were also present in Madagascar, Burma, Sicily, Italy and north west Europe. With such a record it is hardly surprising that few other regiments can match such a glittering list of battle honours.

Officer of the 21st, *c.* 1776

The origins of the 71st Highland Light Infantry are to be found in the regiment raised in 1777 by John Mackenzie, the eldest son of the Earl of Cromarty. He was officially styled 'John Mackenzie, known as Lord Macleod' because although he had been stripped of his title following his involvement with the Jacobites during the unsuccessful '45 Rising, he was still known as a lord to his clansmen. Therefore, he adopted this rather unusual official styling which did not contradict his status in law but which recognised his standing among his own people. The regiment was was originally raised as the 73rd but in 1786 it was assigned the vacant number of 71 which it retained until its subsequent amalgamation with the 74th.

The 74th Highlanders was raised in 1787. Their first colonel was Major General

Sir Archibald Campbell of Inverneil. Both the 71st and the 74th were raised for government service as Highland regiments, but recruiting difficulties in the Highlands led them to seek men in Glasgow and the Lowlands. Originally, both these regiments were kilted. In 1809, the 71st were granted the distinction of being entitled the 71st (Highland Light Infantry) Regiment and wore trews, while in the same year, the 74th lost Highland status and ceased to wear tartan altogether.

Both regiments, who were to be linked in 1881 to form the 1st and 2nd Battalions of the Highland Light Infantry, saw extensive service in Gibraltar, India, The Cape of Good Hope, Buenos Aires, The Peninsula Campaign and Waterloo. No other regiment had more Peninsular battle honours on its colours than the 74th Highlanders.

Major John Potter M.C. with Iraqi prisoners, Kuwait 1991

After 1881 and the formation of the 1st and 2nd Battalions of the Highland Light Infantry, the record of each battalion was equally outstanding at the Battle of Tel-El-Kebir (1882), during the Boer War, and during both the First and Second World Wars. Finally, when the strands were drawn together with the amalgamation of The Royal Scots Fusiliers in 1959, there was created the highly honoured and uniquely distinguished regiment of The Royal Highland Fusiliers.

Since 1959, The Royal Highland Fusiliers have seen service in many parts of the world including Aden, Malta, Germany, Cyprus, Gibralter, Northern Ireland and Singapore. The regiment gained new laurels during the battle for Kuwait in 1991, when one of its officers, Major John Potter, who was serving as a company commander with The Royal Scots during the advance, was awarded the Military Cross.

Origins of the Regiment

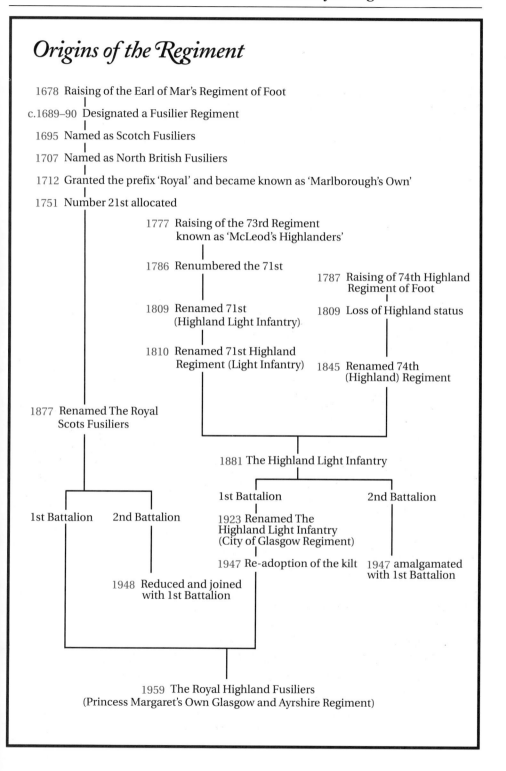

1678 Raising of the Earl of Mar's Regiment of Foot

c.1689–90 Designated a Fusilier Regiment

1695 Named as Scotch Fusiliers

1707 Named as North British Fusiliers

1712 Granted the prefix 'Royal' and became known as 'Marlborough's Own'

1751 Number 21st allocated

1777 Raising of the 73rd Regiment known as 'McLeod's Highlanders'

1786 Renumbered the 71st

1787 Raising of 74th Highland Regiment of Foot

1809 Renamed 71st (Highland Light Infantry)

1809 Loss of Highland status

1810 Renamed 71st Highland Regiment (Light Infantry)

1845 Renamed 74th (Highland) Regiment

1877 Renamed The Royal Scots Fusiliers

1881 The Highland Light Infantry

1st Battalion

2nd Battalion

1st Battalion 2nd Battalion

1923 Renamed The Highland Light Infantry (City of Glasgow Regiment)

1947 Re-adoption of the kilt

1947 amalgamated with 1st Battalion

1948 Reduced and joined with 1st Battalion

1959 The Royal Highland Fusiliers
(Princess Margaret's Own Glasgow and Ayrshire Regiment)

Orders of dress 1961

Tartans

The Royal Highland Fusiliers faithfully preserve part of their history in the two tartans worn by the regiment, the Mackenzie and the dress Erskine.

The Royal Scots Fusiliers did not wear tartan until 1881, a factor which makes them no less Scottish. By 1881, however, the wearing of tartan was so popular all over Scotland, not just in the Highlands, that the major army reorganisations in that year were used to introduce tartan into Lowland regiments. In addition, both the Scots Guards and The Royal Scots Fusiliers were offered the opportunity to wear Government tartan trews. The Royal Scots Fusiliers objected strongly to this without success, but after 1901 they adopted their own tartan, the Government or Black Watch tartan sett with a blue line added.

In 1928 to commemorate the 250th anniversary of the regiment, The Royal Scots Fusiliers pipers were permitted by King George V to wear the dress Erskine, Erskine being the family name of the Earl of Mar. After the Second World War and with the amalgamation of the 1st and 2nd Battalions of The Royal Scots Fusiliers, the regiment adopted trews of hunting Erskine while the pipers retained the dress Erskine. The regiment wore Hunting Erskine until its amalgamation with The Highland Light Infantry.

When they were raised in 1777, the 71st wore kilts and plaids of Government or Black Watch tartan. Very shortly afterwards a buff and red and later a white and red stripe was added to this and the result came to be known as the Mackenzie tartan, after their Colonel John Mackenzie, Lord McLeod. Trews of the same tartan were worn by the 71st after 1809 when they were designated light infantry.

Mackenzie tartan

Erskine tartan

61

The 74th Highland Regiment wore kilts and plaids of Government tartan from the time that they were raised in 1787. The regiment ceased to wear any tartan in 1809, but as the result of a persistent and sustained campaign led by their commanding officer, Lieutenant Colonel Crabbe, the 74th were again designated 'Highland' after 1845 and adopted the Government tartan with a white stripe, called the Lamont tartan, despite the regiment having no connection with the Lamont name or family. This tartan was also known as the 74th tartan and was worn by the 74th Highlanders until they joined the 71st in 1881 and became the 2nd Battalion Highland Light Infantry which then adopted the Mackenzie tartan trews.

Private, 1992

For many years the Highland Light Infantry laid claim to the kilt and tried to have it restored to the regiment. Although trews had originally been just as much the mark of a Highlander as the kilt, the adoption of trews by Lowland regiments in 1881 was considered by many to have devalued trews as Highland garb. The HLI's campaign to restore the kilt was finally successful in 1947. Thus, by the time the Royal Scots Fusiliers and the Highland Light Infantry were amalgamated in 1959 the former wore trews of hunting Erskine and the latter wore kilts of Mackenzie tartan. Amongst the many complex and difficult problems to be resolved following the amalgamation was the question of tartans; the solution was found in the new regiment wearing trews of Mackenzie tartan with the pipers in kilts of dress Erskine.

Clan or Scottish Family Affiliations

All three component parts of the Royal Highland Fusiliers have strong clan associations. The Royal Scots Fusiliers are associated with the ancient Barony of Erskine in Renfrewshire, which was linked by marriage to the Celtic earldom and chieftainship of the 'tribe and lands' of Mar. When the Royal Scots Fusiliers were raised in 1678, however, they were not formed as a clan or Highland regiment but much more as an anti-Covenanter, loyalist regiment.

The 71st were a Mackenzie regiment, having been raised by John Mackenzie, Lord Macleod, the elder son of the Earl of Cromarty. John Mackenzie was an unusual and accomplished man. He had been imprisoned in the Tower of London after the 1745 Rebellion, but was released because of his youth. He travelled to Sweden, where he joined the Swedish Army and became an extremely distinguished soldier, rising to the rank of general. At the outbreak of the American War of Independence he offered his services to King George III. Most of his men came from his old estates on the Moray Firth and the Cromarty Firth. The remainder were recruited in Glasgow, beginning the regiment's long association with that city to which so many Highland men migrated over the centuries.

The 74th, whose first colonel was Sir Archibald Campbell of Inverneil, was raised as a Campbell regiment and ordered to be recruited from the Highlands as a Highland regiment specifically for service in India. The colonelcy of the regiment was actually gifted to Sir Archibald as a reward for services to the crown. He was a distinguished engineering officer who had first come to notice as a result of his service during the American War of Independence and in 1787 was serving as Governor and Commander-in-Chief at Madras in India. However, he took no part in the actual raising of the 74th, a task entrusted to his two brothers James and Duncan Campbell. The raising order of the 74th is dated the 12 October 1787 and the regiment was expected to be ready with over 1000 recruits by Christmas of the same year, a task that was practically impossible from the outset. However, aided by the consent of the Duke of Argyll to recruit on Campbell Lands, the gathering of men and the appointment of officers began with men being recruited as far afield as Appin, Lochaber and Aberdeenshire. Already behind schedule and still short of men, the recruits marched to Glasgow in January 1788 recruiting on the way.

Only half of the alloted 1000 men had been gathered together in Glasgow when four companies were ordered to India and it was not until June 1789, in India, that the 74th were completed and inspected as one body. Sir Archibald Campbell never saw his regiment. As the 74th sailed to India he sailed home were he died in 1791.

Battle Honours

The great battle honours of The Royal Highland Fusiliers serve as a witness to 300 years of loyal service and rugged endeavour. Such service at the Battle of Assaye in India in 1803 earned the 74th Highlanders not only the title the 'Assaye Regiment' but also a third colour, presented to them by the Honourable East India Company, a version of which is still carried on parade today by The Royal Highland Fusiliers.

Alongside that of Assaye stands the distinguished battle honour 'Blenheim', awarded to the 21st Royal Scots Fusiliers in 1704 for its part in this the first of the great battles of The War of the Spanish Succession (1701-14). The French under Louis XIV of France laid claim to the throne of Spain and its territories (which then included part of present-day Netherlands) in the hope of dominating Europe. The combined armies of France and Bavaria were opposed by the army of the Grand Alliance of Britain, Holland, Austria and several German states, led by John Churchill, 1st Duke of Marlborough. Initially, the experienced and disciplined French army was successful in capturing much of the Low Countries and in threatening Vienna, the Austrian capital. Marching from the Low Countries, Marlborough led his armies across the Rhine and surprised the French and Bavarian armies near the village of Blenheim on the River Danube. Each army was approximately 50,000 strong. Daring, resolute and probably one of the greatest soldiers who ever lived, Marlborough determined to attack at once. To achieve victory it was necessary that he break through the enemy's centre, but to do this he had to contain part of the French army in the village of Blenheim. The colonel of the 21st Royal Scots Fusiliers, Brigadier Archibald Row, was chosen to lead the frontal attack on the village. With four other battalions, the 21st advanced against an enemy vastly superior in numbers and fortified in the village by hedges, a palisade and a series of complex defences.

By this stage in the campaign the 21st were tired and far from home, having marched half way across Europe. With resigned determination, they advanced across the open fields in front of the palisade, holding their fire. When they were only 30 paces away the enemy fired a volley straight into them. One third of the men fell but the advance continued. Only when they were actually at the palisade did the 21st open fire and an heroic and desperate hand-to-hand struggle began. In the ensuing struggle, Brigadier Row, the commanding officer, and the second-in-command were all killed. Eventually, allied reinforcements arrived and the 21st and others managed to secure ground to cover the exits to the village of Blenheim. Marlborough made a completely successful attack on the French centre and the enemy inside Blenheim were surrounded, losing in all about 40,000 men killed, wounded, and captured.

Many of the battle honours of the Royal Highland Fusiliers are much less well known than Blenheim, but just as deserving of mention. One such honour is 'South Africa 1851–53' earned by the 74th Highlanders over two years of marching and battles, fighting not only a skilled and elusive enemy, but also dysentery, bronchitis, extremes of temperature, and flies. During this campaign, the 74th adapted their dress to broad brimmed hats or 'wide awakes' and brown canvas jackets, but they

The 74th Highlanders at Krome Heights during the Kaffir War, 1851

The 74th Highlanders at the Battle of Assaye, India, 1803 (Reproduced by permission of David Rowlar

kept their Lamont tartan trews which earned them their nickname of 'Tortoises': the white stripe of the trews was similar to the stripe on the back of the tortoises which abounded in the Amatola Mountains to the north of Port Elizabeth in South Africa where the campaign was fought.

Two well-known and much-loved men of the 74th died in South Africa during this campaign, Lieutenant Colonel Jock Fordyce and Band Master Hartung. It was still relatively common and indeed fashionable in British regiments in the 1840s and '50s to have civilian German band masters. Their musical abilities were considered superior to those of any other nation's and these men, although civilians and paid for by the officers of the regiment, sometimes accompanied their regiment overseas on campaign, as did Band Master Hartung of the 74th Highlanders. By all accounts he was an able musician, a gentle man and much loved in the regiment. However, in an action near Waterkloof, Hartung was taken prisoner by the Kaffirs. He was subsequently murdered and his body was never recovered.

Royal Scots Fusiliers defending Jemappes Bridge during the Battle of Mons, 1914

However, battle honours do not always tell the full story of a regiment's fortitude, perseverance and service. To the honours of the Royal Highland Fusiliers have to be added the many dangers, the long hours on the march, their exemplary conduct at the sinking of the troop ship Birkenhead in 1852 and their tireless contribution to the location of bodies and wreckage after the bringing down of Pan Am Flight 103 in December 1988 at Lockerbie in the Scottish borders. For this latter duty, carried out over a huge tract of countryside with great tact and consideration, the regiment was awarded the Wilkinson Sword of Peace.

Victoria Cross Winners

Private G. Rodgers	71st Highland (Light Infantry)	1858	Indian Mutiny
Lt. W.M.M. Edwards	2nd Bn Highland Light Infantry	1882	Egypt
Cpl A.G. Hore-Ruthven	3rd Bn Highland light Infantry	1898	Sudan
Private G. Ravenhill	2nd Bn Royals Scots Fusiliers	1899	South Africa
Capt. J. Shaul	1st Bn Highland Light Infantry	1899	South Africa
Private C. Kennedy	1st Bn Highland Light Infantry	1900	SouthAfrica
Private G. Wilson	2nd Bn Highland Light Infantry	1914	Western Front
Lt W.L. Brodie	2nd Bn Highland Light Infantry	1914	Western Front
L/Cpl W. Angus	8th Bn Highland Light Infantry	1915	Western Front
Private R. Lauder	4th Bn Royal Scots Fusiliers	1915	Gallipoli
Sgt J.Y. Turnbull	17th Bn Highland Light Infantry	1916	Western Front
Lt. W. Honey, M.C., M.M.	Highland Light Infantry of Canada	1917	Western Front
2nd Lt. J.M. Craig	5th Bn Royal Scots Fusiliers	1917	Gaza
2nd Lt. S.H.P. Boughey	4th Bn Royal Scots Fusiliers	1917	Jerusalem
L/Cpl J.B. Hamilton	9th Bn Highland Light Infantry	1917	Western Front
Sgt. T. Caldwell	12th Bn Royal Scots Fusiliers	1918	Western Front
Lt Col. W.H. Anderson	12th Bn Highland Light Infantry	1918	Western Front
Cpl D.F. Hunter	5th Bn Highland Light Infantry	1918	Western Front
Major F.G. Blaker, M.C.	Highland Light Infantry	1944	Burma
Fus. D. Donnini	4th/5th Bn Royal Scots Fusiliers	1945	Germany

Lt W. Brodie V.C.

The Royal Highland Fusiliers can proudly lay claim to 20 Victoria Cross Winners between 1858 and 1945, a remarkable achievement by any standard. One of these winners of the British Army's premier award for bravery in action was Captain Walter Lorrain Brodie of the 2nd Battalion Highland Light Infantry. Walter Brodie was born in Edinburgh in 1884, the son of a chartered accountant. His school days were spent at Edinburgh Academy after which he went to Sandhurst and joined his regiment. The 2nd Battalion the Highland Light Infantry landed in France on 14th August 1914 and they had already taken part in the great battles of the retreat from Mons and the Aisne when they were sent to the area of Ypres in Belgium to hold the determined German advance to the sea. Most of the fields were still green in the late autumn mist, the woods and houses still standing. In some places the imperfect and often shallow trenches were only 50 yards apart. At 4.30 a.m. on 11th November 1914 a party of 300 Germans succeeded in getting into the trenches held by the Highland Light Infantry. As the alarm sounded the HLI men, according to a pre-arranged plan, scrambled out of their trench to the rear and took shelter behind the parados. From this position they launched themselves upon the enemy; in the fiece hand-to-hand fighting that followed the Scots were heavily outnumbered and in the mist and darkness, it was every man for himself. The HLI's machine guns were overrun and Brodie, the machine-gun officer, seized a rifle and, shouting desperately above the deafening noise, led a fighting bayonet charge to recapture the trench. With the help of his men, he succeeded in recapturing and mounting one of the machine guns, firing it down the line of the occupied trench.

As the mist cleared and the dawn broke, the intensity of the early morning struggle became apparent. Eighty of the enemy lay dead, many in the trench itself and 51 had been taken prisoner. Modestly, Brodie described this desperate fighting simply as a 'bit of a scrap'. Walter Brodie served on through the war and was commanding his battalion by 1918. He had, in fact, never left the 2nd Battalion Highland Light Infantry since they arrived in France in 1914, apart from leave to recover from wounds. He was loved and respected in the battalion and considered by his men to be a good luck symbol with a charmed life. Sadly, however, Brodie died leading his men in the Battle of Albert on 23rd August 1918 less than three months before the war ended.

Regimental Pipe Music

Quick marches	*Highland Laddie* *All the Blue Bonnets are over the Border*
March past in slow time	*My Home*
Company March	
A Company	*The Mucking of Geordie's Byre*
B Company	*The Bugle Horn*
C Company	*McDonald's Awa to the Wars*
D Company	*Bonnie Dundee*
S Company	*Orange and Blue*
Headquarter Company	*Scotland The Brave*
Funerals	*Lochaber no More*
Regimental Guest Night	*Highland Laddie* *The 71st's Quick Step* *The 74th's Slow March*

Pipe Major Gavin Stoddart, winner of the 1981 London Bicentenary Gold Medal

The Royal Highland Fusiliers have a long tradition in pipe playing and also in Highland dancing. Although the 74th Highlanders lost Highland status for a period during their history they seemed to have firmly maintained the tradition of keeping their pipers. Included in the lists of the Highlands Society of London's Gold Medal Winners are William MacKinnon of the 74th and Pipe Major Matheson of the Highland Light Infantry. In more recent times the Royal Highland Fusiliers have achieved outstanding piping success through the talented playing of Captain Gavin N.M. Stoddart BEM, promoted from Pipe Major to become Director of Army Bagpipe Music at the Army School of Piping, Edinburgh Castle.

Regimental pipers have also been consistently picked out for their individual bravery in action, such as Piper George Clark of the 71st at Vimiera during the Peninsular Campaign of 1808 who, although wounded and unable to go any further, played on his comrades into the attack.

As for the regimental tunes themselves, there is probably no more evocative sight and sound than sitting at dinner in the Royal Highland Fusiliers Officers' Mess, the colours in their stand, the silver on the table glittering in the candlelight, listening to the strains of the pipes as the pipers circle the table for the last time to the old tune, *The 74th's Slow March* or *The Bellisle March*, an old fife tune. Only when the sound has completely died away in the distance is the spell broken and the applause accorded to the players.

Allied and Affiliated Regiments

Canada   The Highland Fusiliers of Canada
New Zealand   1st Battalion Royal New Zealand Infantry Regiment
Pakistan   11th Battalion the Baluch Regiment
South Africa   Prince Alfred's Guard

The 71st Highlanders in Canada, 1838

Piper George Clark at the Battle of Vimiera, 1808

The King's Own Scottish Borderers

The King's Own Scottish Borderers has an unusual history. It is one of only two Scottish regiments which have not been amalgamated with any other regiment and although raised in Edinburgh in 1689, the regiment lost its Scottish name between 1782 and 1805 when it was known as the 25th (Sussex) Regiment of Foot. It was not until 1887 that the regiment assumed its present title, and since that date, it has secured its place in the heart of Border Scots. The regiment is most often known by the initials, K.O.S.B. Throughout its history, the regiment has served with considerable bravery in the service of its country from the siege of Namur in 1695 to the battlefields of Korea in 1952, and the Gulf in 1991.

In 1991, plans were announced for the amalgamation of the regiment with The Royal Scots. Fortunately, this unpopular move was abandoned early in 1993 following a re-assessment of future force requirements.

Badge

The badge of The King's Own Scottish Borderers is represented by, upon a saltire, the Castle of Edinburgh, with mottoes *In veritate religionis confido* (I trust in the truth of my belief) and *Nisi dominus frustra* (In vain without the Lord), all ensigned with the royal crest.

The badge strongly reflects the Scottish, and particularly Edinburgh, origins of the regiment. Raised in 1689 when Scotland was on the brink of civil war and tension in the city ran high, the

Convention of Estates agreed to accept William of Orange and the Protestant succession. A proclamation was issued to secure the defence of their decision:

The meeting of the Estates of the kingdome of Scotland doe order and warrand the Earle of Levin to cause, beat drums and call together all persones who will assist him and joyne with the train bands to secure that no men be put into the Castle of Edinburgh and no persone be suffered to sallie forth thereof and to dissipat any persones who may be together in armes without warrand of the Estates and to secure the peace of the Toune.

Within two hours, 800 men had joined Leven's regiment and the castle, the thistles and the saltire of the badge serve as a permanent reminder of these historic events.

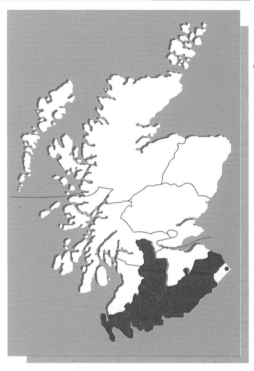

Regimental Recruiting Area

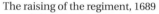
The raising of the regiment, 1689

The Battle of Killiecrankie, 1689

Regimental Origin

Set against a background of political turmoil, Leven's regiment, known as the Edinburgh Regiment, was raised in 1689 for the defence of the capital city and to secure the Protestant succession to the throne in Scotland. At the time, Edinburgh Castle was held by the Duke of Gordon for the Catholic monarch, James II, and Graham of Claverhouse, Viscount Dundee was attempting to rally the nobility and elements of the Highland clans to fight for King James.

During the first days of their service, the men of the Earl of Leven's regiment set about digging trenches in several parts of the city. In the end, the Duke of Gordon was forced to capitulate and Leven's regiment was free to move into Fife and thence on to Killiecrankie. There, on 27th July 1689, they faced Dundee's Highlanders in the wooded braes of the narrow pass. Although Dundee secured a famous victory, Leven's regiment was one of only two which withstood the wild Highland charge. Despite this victory, Dundee was mortally wounded and the Highlanders failed to exploit their advantage. In recognition of their outstanding performance at the battle of Killiecrankie, the Scottish capital honoured its regiment by granting it the unique privilege of recruiting in the city by beat of drum on any day except Sunday, without securing permission.

David Leslie, 3rd Earl of Leven

After service in Ireland, the regiment fought in the War of the League of Augsburg (1688-97) from 1692 and was present at the battles of Steenkirk (1692) and Landen (1693) and the siege at Namur (1695).

The Edinburgh Regiment fought for the government against the Jacobites at Sheriffmuir in 1715. In 1743, they proceeded to the continent to take part in the War of the Austrian Succession (1740-48) and fought at Fontenoy (1745). However, they returned hurriedly to garrison Edinburgh Castle against the Jacobites, later taking part in the battle of Culloden (1746) under Cumberland's command.

After the suppression of the Jacobite rebellion, they again returned to the continent and in 1751 were designated the 25th (Edinburgh) Regiment of Foot. They then served in the Seven Years' War (1756-63) where on 1st August 1759, along with five other British regiments, they fought against the French at the Battle of Minden. As the 25th advanced into battle, the soldiers picked wild roses to put in their hats as a means of identification. In commemoration, the members of the regiment wear roses in their head-dress on Minden Day each year.

In 1782, the name of the regiment was altered to the 25th (Sussex) Regiment. Lord George Lennox was the colonel at the time, and his family seat was at Goodwood in Sussex.

During the French Revolutionary Wars, the 25th furnished detachments of men to serve as Marines and these contingents fought with Admiral Lord Howe's Squadron. By 1795, the regiment had sailed for Grenada, returning in 1799 to take part in raids on the Dutch Coast. The men distinguished themselves particularly in operations at Egmont-Op-Zee.

After service in Egypt, for which the 25th were rewarded with the Sphinx super-scribed 'Egypt, the regiment returned to England and was named 25th (The King's Own Borderers) Regiment of Foot in 1805. Under their new name, they took part in the capture of Martinique (1809) and Guadeloupe (1810).

After numerous duties world-wide, The King's Own Borderers served in India from 1868 until 1889. They joined the Peshawar Valley Field Force during the Second Afghan War, advancing beyond Fort Jamrud and through the Khyber Pass.

In the army reorganisations of 1881, it was decided, apparently arbitrarily, to call the regiment the York Regiment, King's Own Borderers and to move the regimental depot to York. Amid a storm of protest, the English appellation was dropped and the depot was instead relocated at Berwick-upon-Tweed. In 1887, the regiment was renamed The King's Own Scottish Borderers, with two battalions.

The 1st Battalion fought in Burma in 1889 while the 2nd Battalion served in Sudan, later moving to India in 1895 to join the Chitral Relief Force on the North West Frontier. The 2nd Battalion also served in the Tirah alongside The Gordon Highlanders.

In 1889, the 1st Battalion The King's Own Scottish Borderers moved to South Africa to fight in the 2nd Boer War. During the First World War the regiment raised a total of twelve battalions fighting from the early days of the retreat from Mons to Ypres; at the Somme, Delville Wood, Arras, and Vimy Ridge; the landings at Gallipoli; in Gaza and in Palestine.

On the outbreak of the Second World War, the 2nd Battalion landed in France and formed part of the 9th Brigade, under Major General B. L. Montgomery. After stiff fighting and an exhausting retreat, the regiment was finally evacuated from the sands of Bray-Dunes, some ten miles from Dunkirk. Throughout the Second World War, The King's Own Scottish Borderers achieved distinction in north west Europe, in Burma and the Arakan, at the Normandy landings, at Arnhem, and at the great battle in the Reichswald Forest.

The K.O.S.B. at Maiden in the Tirah, India, 1897

In 1947, the 2nd Battalion The King's Own Scottish Borderers was disbanded. The 1st Battalion went on to achieve particular distinction during the Korean War, which began in June 1950. During this conflict, Private William Speakman (serving with The Black Watch but who at the time was attached to the 1st Battalion) was awarded the Victoria Cross. After Korea, the regiment served throughout the world, including Northern Ireland, Malaya, Germany, Aden, the Radfan and in Borneo. More recently, it played a role in the Gulf War.

Left Corporal, 1992
Below The K.O.S.B. in Canada, 1864

Origins of the Regiment

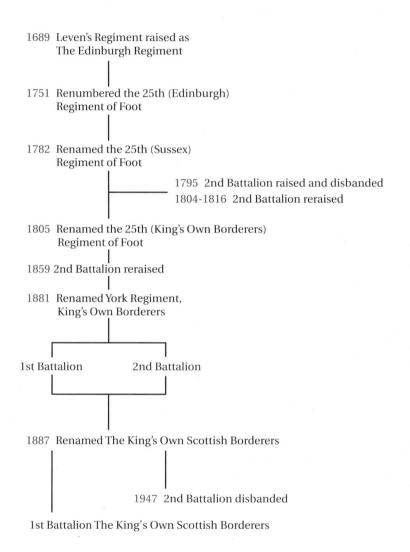

1689 Leven's Regiment raised as
The Edinburgh Regiment

1751 Renumbered the 25th (Edinburgh)
Regiment of Foot

1782 Renamed the 25th (Sussex)
Regiment of Foot

1795 2nd Battalion raised and disbanded
1804-1816 2nd Battalion reraised

1805 Renamed the 25th (King's Own Borderers)
Regiment of Foot

1859 2nd Battalion reraised

1881 Renamed York Regiment,
King's Own Borderers

1st Battalion   2nd Battalion

1887 Renamed The King's Own Scottish Borderers

1947 2nd Battalion disbanded

1st Battalion The King's Own Scottish Borderers

Tartans

The King's Own Scottish Borderers did not wear tartan until 1882, when permission was given, in common with other Lowland regiments, to wear trews of Government, or Black Watch, tartan. The wearing of the distinctive Leslie tartan as trews in honour of the Earl of Leven was not authorised until 1898, and even these were not issued to the rank and file until 1904. The regimental pipers wear Royal Stewart tartan kilts.

Leslie tartan   Royal Stewart tartan

Clan or Scottish Family Affiliations

The King's Own Scottish Borderers take great pride in their affiliation with the Earl of Leven and the Leslie family. The Earl of Leven and Melville is chief of the ancient family of Melville which claim descent from an Anglo-Norman family which settled in the Edinburgh area during the reign of David I. Equally, the family has connections with Germany, France, Hungary, Russia and Poland. David Leslie, 3rd Earl of Leven was a distinguished and experienced soldier who returned to Britain with Prince William of Orange and raised the regiment.

Battle Honours

Amongst all the battle honours earned by the 25th of Foot The King's Own Scottish Borderers, the most notable is 'Minden'. Only five other regiments in the British army hold this particular honour.

On 1st August 1759, a battle took place on the banks of the River Weser, near the fortified town of Minden. Ferdinand, Duke of Brunswick commanded contingents from Britain and from the German states, numbering nearly 80,000 men, against two French armies, numbering almost 97,000.

The plans of both Ferdinand and the French commander, Contades, were set aside, when a regiment of Ferdinand's army advanced to the attack unsupported, having apparently mistaken their orders. Immediately, the six British regiments and a battalion of Hanoverian guards were completely exposed, and as Ferdinand's line advanced in response, they were charged by waves of French heavy cavalry. In succession, the mass squadrons of cavalry ran head-long into the British and Hanoverian infantry, who apparently, without heed to the danger which they faced, stood absolutely firm in line, steadily firing volleys of accurate and devastating fire. It was an astonishing feat for unsupported infantry to repel repeated cavalry charges in this way.

The French centre was now broken. Although the British and Hanoverian artillery began to harass the enemy, the cavalry under George, Lord Sackville failed to charge and the French were thus able to extricate themselves, leaving behind some 10,000 men killed, wounded or missing. The battle has become a legend and is part of the continuing story of courage in the face of extreme adversity which runs through the history of the British army. To commemorate this victory, each year Minden Day is celebrated as a regimental day in The King's Own Scottish Borderers.

Regimental Colours

84

Victoria Cross Winners

Lt G. H. B. Coulson	1st Bn K.O.S.B.	1901	Boer War
Piper D. Laidlaw	7th Bn K.O.S.B.	1915	Loos
CSM J. Skinner	1st Bn K.O.S.B.	1917	Ypres
CQMS W. Grimbaldeston	1st Bn K.O.S.B.	1917	Ypres
Sgt L. McGuffie	5th Bn K.O.S.B.	1918	Belgium
Private W. Speakman	1st Bn K.O.S.B.	1951	Korea

Piper D. Laidlaw V.C.

Perhaps one of the most well known stories of the Victoria Cross is that of Piper, later Sergeant Piper, Daniel Laidlaw.

Daniel Laidlaw was born at Little Swinton near Berwick-upon-Tweed on 26th July 1875. At the outbreak of the First World War, he joined the 7th Battalion The King's Own Scottish Borderers. In 1915, the battalion was serving as part of the 15th Scottish Division in the Loos Sector. It was the first time that the battalion had been in action.

On 25th September 1915, just before the British attack on Hill 70 and Loos, the battalion came under heavy artillery fire and poisoned gas. The gas attack severely affected many men and the remainder were visibly shaken. Above the din and confusion of battle, the commanding officer, seeing Piper Laidlaw with his pipes, shouted above the noise, 'Pipe them together Laidlaw, for God's sake, pipe them together'.

With complete disregard for his own safety, Daniel Laidlaw got up onto the parapet of the trench and played his comrades into action in full view of the enemy. In the face of heavy machine-gun fire and to the sound of *Blue Bonnets o'er the Border* and *The Standard on the Braes o' Mar*, the Borderers went forward with stoic determination to attack the German trenches. Although wounded before he reached the German line, Laidlaw was awarded the Victoria Cross and the French Croix de Guerre for his conspicuous gallantry.

Although Piper Laidlaw acquired the nickname 'The Piper of Loos', he was not the only player to achieve this distinction. He was quick, however, to give credit to the other pipers who had played during the battle, and who had also rendered extraordinary service in great danger by bringing in the wounded. In particular, Pipe Major Douglas Taylor, although wounded in the hand and unable to pipe, continued to bring in wounded men from the battlefield for 36 hours.

Daniel Laidlaw died at Shoresdean, near Berwick-upon-Tweed, on 2nd June 1950 and is buried at Norham.

Regimental Music

Pipe Marches

March in quick time	*Blue Bonnets o'er the Border*
March in slow time	*The Borderers*
The Charge	*The Standard on the Braes o' Mar*

Company Marches

A Company	*The Bugle Horn*
B Company	*Bonnie Dundee*
C Company	*The Mucking o' Geordie's Byre*
Support Company	*A Liberton Polka*
Headquarter Company	*Cock o' the North*

Regimental Band

March in slow time	*The Garb of Auld Gaul*

Allied and Affiliated Regiments

Canada

1st Battalion The Royal New Brunswick Regiment (Carleton & York)

Australia

25th Battalion The Royal Queensland Regiment

Malaysia

5th Battalion The Royal Malay Regiment

The Cameronians

Scottish Rifles

This remarkable regiment can trace its origins back to 1689, when it was raised under unique circumstances. The regiment is an amalgamation of the 26th Cameronian Regiment and the 90th Perthshire Light Infantry which were brought together, albeit reluctantly, in the Army Reforms of 1881 as The Cameronians (Scottish Rifles). Since then, their recruiting base has been firmly located in Lanarkshire and the Glasgow area, where the 26th Cameronian Regiment originated.

The regiment has an old and distinguished history, particularly in their early battle honours. In 1968, however, in the face of further army reforms, they chose to disband rather than amalgamate. The Cameronians only exist today as detachments of the Army Cadet Force.

Badge

The badge of The Cameronians (Scottish Rifles) is a Mullet of the Coat of Arms of the Douglas family, upon a stringed Bugle Horn, within two sprays of thistles.

The badge reflects the origins of the regiment and its connections with the ancient and powerful Douglas family. It also commemorates their origins in the Light Infantry, as indicated by the bugle horn. Bugles were used in light infantry regiments to give signals in the field in the same way as the drum was used in infantry line regiments. In 1881, the new amalgamated regiment was designated as a rifle regiment.

Regimental Origin

The origin of The Cameronians (Scottish Rifles) is absolutely unique because it is the only regiment in the British army which has a religious foundation. The name 'Cameronian' was given to the most militant of the Presbyterian sects which sought to prevent any dilution of the Presbyterian faith, and who upheld the principles of the National Covenant, signed at Greyfriars Church Yard in Edinburgh on 28th February 1638. The Covenanters were virtually outlawed and they resorted to holding their religious worship in secret locations on hillsides, known as conventicles. After numerous trials, endless debate, and frequent battles, and with the arrival of the Protestant William, Prince of Orange to the throne in November 1688, the

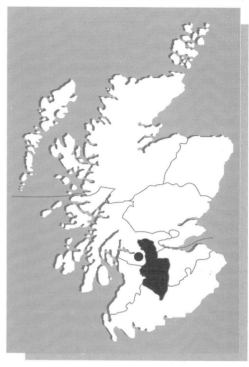

Regimental Recruiting Area

Covenanters were brought into government service as The Cameronian Regiment.

The first muster of the regiment took place at Douglas Parish Kirk, Lanarkshire on 12th May 1689. Here a declaration was read out, and explained to the assembled men:

All shall be well affected, of approved fidelity and of a sober conversation. The cause they are called to appear for, is the service of the King's Majesty and the defence of the Nation, recovery and preservation of the Protestant Religion; and in particular the work of reformation in Scotland, in opposition to Popery, prelacy and arbitrary power in all its branches and steps, until the Government of Church and State be brought back to that lustre and integrity which it had in the best times.

This extraordinary regiment was, therefore, as much a congregation as a military force. Each company had its elder and every man carried a Bible. Traditionally, the regiment posted sentinels at church parades and the sermon did not commence until an officer notified the minister with a shout of 'All clear!'

The young regiment fought with great bravery and distinction against the Highlanders at Dunkeld in 1689, where it was engaged in a ferocious battle in the area of the cathedral, and amongst the buildings and walls of the town. In 1691, they joined William III's Army in the Netherlands and fought in the War of the League of Augsburg at Steenkirk (1692) and Landen (1693).

In 1702, the regiment returned to the continent to fight in the War of Spanish Succession (1701-14). Under the Duke of Marlborough, the Cameronians were present at the capture of Schellenberg (1704) and at Ramillies (1706). In 1709, the regiment, positioned in the centre of the British line, played an important part in the battle of Malplaquet, forcing the French to break and allowing the cavalry to advance.

Private, Cameronian Territorial Company, 1992

The Cameronians garrisoned both Gibraltar and Minorca during the War of the Austrian Succession (1740-48) and in 1751 were renamed the 26th Regiment (The Cameronians). They embarked for the American colonies in 1767. In 1775, they formed detachments at the forts of Ticonderoga and Crown Point and after the British defeat at Saratoga in 1777, the regiment was essentially drafted to other units, only a small group returning home to begin recruiting anew.

With the outbreak of the wars with the French, The Cameronians took part in the landings at Aboukir Bay in 1801 and the capture of Alexandria.

Subsequently, the regiment was present at the retreat to Corunna (1808) and the Walcheren Expedition in the Netherlands. In July 1811, they arrived in Portugal under the command of the Duke of Wellington, where they saw great hardship but little action and were withdrawn to garrison Gibraltar.

The Cameronians took part in the First China War in 1841 and the War in Abyssinia under Lord Napier in 1868.

The 90th Perthshire Light Infantry were raised by the charismatic Thomas Graham of Balgowan, later General Lord Lynedoch, as the 90th Regiment of Foot, or Perthshire Volunteers, in 1794. Sworn by deep personal commitment to devote his life to fighting the French, he raised the regiment at his own expense. A 2nd Battalion was also raised, but these men were drafted to the Marines.

The 90th were known affectionately as the 'Perthshire Grey Breeks' and were designated The Perthshire Volunteers (Light Infantry). Like the 26th Cameronians, they landed at Aboukir Bay in 1801 and then went on to participate in the capture of Martinique (1809) and Guadeloupe (1810), where they captured an eagle standard of the French 80th Regiment. In 1815, they were designated as one of six light infantry regiments and were armed and clothed as such. Duty in the Greek islands was followed by service in Ceylon and South Africa.

In 1854, the 90th Perthshire Light Infantry were moved to the Crimea as reinforcements and in 1855, they took part in the famous attack on the quarries in front of the Redan at Sevastopol. On route to China after the Crimean War, they were diverted to take part in suppressing the Indian Mutiny and were present at the siege and relief of Lucknow. In 1878, they again served in South Africa, in the Zulu Wars.

It was with extreme sadness, and great reluctance that they became the 2nd Battalion The Cameronians (Scottish Rifles) in 1881. Following the amalgamation of the 26th and the 90th to form the 1st and 2nd Battalions of the regiment, it was common practice for many years for the 1st Battalion to refer to themselves as only 'The Cameronians' and for the 2nd to refer to themselves only as 'Scottish Rifles'.

In spite of these difficulties, the regiment served with great distinction during the 2nd Boer War (1889–1902). During the First World War (1914-18), the battle honours 'Mons', 'Marne', 'Neuve Chapelle', 'Ypres' and 'Gallipoli' were amongst the many that were added to the distinguished battle honours already held. In 1940, the 2nd Battalion were evacuated at Dunkirk, having lost 365 of their comrades as casualties. During the Second World War (1939-45), the regiment again earned an enviable reputation in battles as far afield as north west Europe, Italy and Burma.

In 1946, the 1st Battalion were placed in 'suspended animation' and the 2nd Battalion was renumbered as the 1st Battalion. However, as a result of force reductions and army reforms and at their own request, the regiment was disbanded and a last conventicle was held on 14th May 1968.

Tartans

The Cameronians did not wear tartan until 1881 when, in common with other Lowland regiments, they adopted the Government, or Black Watch, tartan. It was only in 1891 that the regiment was authorised to wear the Douglas tartan, which was taken into use the following year. The use of the Douglas tartan reflects the origins of the 26th Cameronian Regiment. In 1881, when the regiment was designated a rifle regiment, the officers and men were clothed in the distinctive Rifle Green cloth with bands of black thistle lace on the shako and black cords. The pipers of the regiment also wore the Douglas tartan.

Douglas tartan

Officers, *c.* 1930

A detachment of Cameronians, Edinburgh, 1953

Clan or Scottish Family Affiliations

The Cameronians (Scottish Rifles) have two distinct affiliations with ancient Scottish families. First, there is the close association to the Douglas family. In 1689, the 26th Cameronian Regiment was raised in the name of the Earl of Angus, the eldest son of the Marquis of Douglas. The origins of this family are ancient, but in the 12th century, their base was to found in Lanarkshire and the family was prominent in the struggle for Scotland's independence. The earldom of Douglas was created in 1357. William, 1st Earl became Earl of Mar by his marriage to Margaret, sister of the 13th Earl of Mar. The half -brother of the 2nd Earl became Earl of Angus, and William, 11th Earl of Angus was created Marquis of Douglas in 1633.

The first colonel of the regiment was the eighteen-year-old James, Earl of Angus, son of the Marquis of Douglas. For a time, the 26th regiment was known as the Lord Angus Regiment. The association with the Douglas family has remained constant throughout the history of the regiment.

The second great family with which The Cameronians is associated is that of Thomas Graham of Balgowan, later General Lord Lynedoch. Thomas Graham (1750-1843) came from Balgowan in Perthshire. This ancient Scottish family can claim amongst its number the Marquis of Montrose and John Graham of Claverhouse, Viscount Dundee.

Thomas Graham was an extraordinary man, with a personal commitment to fight the French. He married the beautiful Catherine, second daughter of Lord Cathcart. She was frequently in ill health and spent a great deal of time abroad. During the French Revolutionary Wars, she died on the Mediterranean coast in France and her husband brought her body back to be buried in Scotland. At Toulouse, the revolutionaries suspected Thomas Graham of smuggling arms and burst open the coffin to examine the contents. Mortally insulted, he vowed to devote the rest of his life to fighting the French. Thomas Graham was created Lord Lynedoch for his services in the Peninsula War.

Battle Honours

As a result of its unique and ancient origin, part of which emanates from the use of light or skirmishing troops, The Cameronians (Scottish Rifles) have some unusual battle honours. One in particular, 'Corunna', stands out in the annals of the regiment.

The 26th Cameronians had been sent to northern Spain in 1808. Napoleon's intention was to sweep across the Iberian Peninsula to Lisbon to deal quickly with the Spanish and British. When he reached Madrid, Napoleon decided to move northwards in order to destroy the British army under General Sir John Moore. In the face of overwhelming odds, Moore's 17,000 men were forced to retreat. Outnumbered, inadequately supplied and without Spanish support, the withdrawal through the mountains of Galicia was a nightmare, exacerbated by bitter rear-guard

Origins of the Regiment

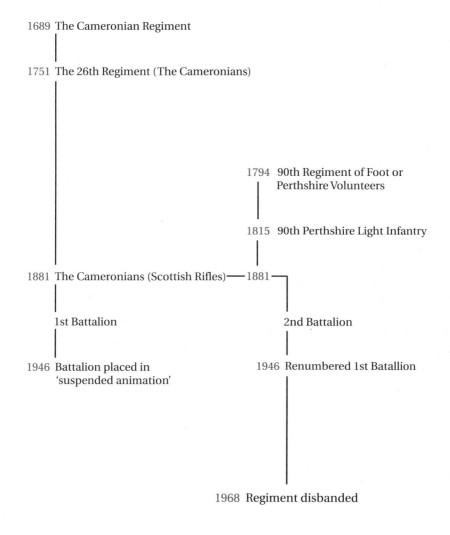

1689 The Cameronian Regiment

1751 The 26th Regiment (The Cameronians)

1794 90th Regiment of Foot or
      Perthshire Volunteers

1815 90th Perthshire Light Infantry

1881 The Cameronians (Scottish Rifles) —— 1881

1st Battalion

2nd Battalion

1946 Battalion placed in
      'suspended animation'

1946 Renumbered 1st Batallion

1968 Regiment disbanded

actions. Corunna, a small port on the north-western extremity of the Iberian peninsula, was reached on 11th January 1809. About 5000 men had been lost during the retreat.

The French attacks began on 16th January and The Cameronians, as part of Moore's reserves, fought with considerable bravery, repelling the French attempts to break the British right. The meagre numbers of British defenders repulsed over 20,000 Frenchman. As a result of the considerable skill of General Sir John Moore, who was fatally wounded in the defence, the British were able to embark and return to England.

General Sir John Moore was an able, distinguished and charismatic soldier who was held in high esteem by his troops. He had served in the American Revolution and in Holland. In Egypt,he distinguishing himself at the landings at Aboukir Bay and at Alexandria (1801). His command in Spain was plagued by a shortage of men, the weather, inadequate supplies and poor relations with his Spanish allies. Despite these difficulties, the retreat to Corunna was conducted with considerable skill. He was buried by his men on the ramparts of that town, and has become a legend in the annals of British military history. The Cameronians have always considered it a distinction to have served under such an able soldier.

Victoria Cross Winners

Private J. Alexander	90th Perthshire Light Infantry	1855	Crimea
Capt. A. Moynihan	90th Perthshire Light Infantry	1855	Crimea
Cpl W. Bradshaw	90th Perthshire Light Infantry	1857	India
Private P. Graham	90th Perthshire Light Infantry	1857	India
Sgt S. Hill	90th Perthshire Light Infantry	1857	India
Surgeon A. Dixon Home	90th Perthshire Light Infantry	1857	India
Lt W. Rennie	90th Perthshire Light Infantry	1857	India
CSgt E. J. Fowler	2nd Bn The Cameronians (Scottish Rifles)	1879	Zulu Land
Col. H. Lysons	2nd Bn The Cameronians (Scottish Rifles)	1879	Zulu Land
Private H. May	1st Bn The Cameronians (Scottish Rifles)	1914	France
Sgt J. Erskine	5th Bn The Cameronians (Scottish Rifles)	1916	France
Private J. Towers	2nd Bn The Cameronians (Scottish Rifles)	1918	France

Sgt J. Erskine V.C.

The modest heroism associated with many Victoria Cross winners is exemplified in the poignant story of one member of The Cameronians, John Erskine.

John Erskine was born in Dunfermline on 13th January 1894. His father worked in a firm of Dunfermline drapers and his mother had been a teacher at Bathgate Academy. A member of a close knit and well-respected family, John was educated at Dunfermline High School and went on to serve his apprenticeship as a draper. By 1914, he was working in Glasgow. Six days after war was declared, he enlisted in the 5th Battalion The Cameronians (Scottish Rifles) and was sent to France in November.

The 5th Battalion was originally formed in 1859-60 as the 1st Lanarkshire Rifle Volunteer Corps, one of the companies of the corps being raised as the University of Glasgow Company. They became a volunteer battalion of The Cameronians in 1881 and, subsequently, many men from the battalion fought in the South African War.

Throughout the First World War, the battalion served on the Western Front. John Erskine, like many who served with him, had many trials and narrow escapes. He was an educated and sensitive man and his regular letters to his family show that he soon became an experienced and conscientious soldier, who particularly cared about the welfare of his brother, Willie.

In late June 1916, the battalion was serving in the area of Givenchy in France. In the chalk soil north of the infamous Hohenzollern Redoubt, both sides had attempted to mine under the trenches, and in some areas there were huge craters caused by the destruction of these mines. The possession of the crater and the lips of the crater was crucial, and on 22nd June 1916, the 5th Battalion The Cameronians were trying to consolidate their position on their side of one such crater. The fire was deafening and intense, when from a position in the rear, John Erskine saw a sergeant and a rifleman, both of whom were wounded, isolated and exposed. Apparently without any hesitation and in the face of a terrific fusillade, he rushed forward and brought in the two wounded men. Later, while the position was still under heavy fire, Erskine went out again after one of his officers, lying in open ground, showed signs of life. Moving forward, he found the officer to be alive. Erskine bandaged his head and remained with him, protecting the wounded man's body with his own, until a shallow trench was dug to them, over an hour later. During the evacuation, John Erskine ensured that his own body was between that of his officer and enemy fire.

Two days later, John Erskine was promoted Lance-Sergeant and he wrote to his family in a matter-of-fact way with no direct reference to his own personal heroism. Lance-Sergeant Erskine's triumph, however, was reported in all the Scottish papers and he became a local hero in Dunfermline and Bathgate. The only reference he made to his award was a request some two months after the event for some V.C. ribbon to be sent to him in France.

Consistently throughout this period, John showed considerable concern for his brother, Willie, then also serving in France. It was indeed a bitter blow when Willie was killed in action on the morning of Saturday, 18th November 1916. John was deeply affected by this loss and before going into action in April 1917, he wrote to his mother:

> I am writing this letter while I have yet time, as I am probably going into action in a day or two. If nothing happens, then you won't get it. Well I can say quite honestly, that I am not in the least afraid to die and I hope you won't be thinking that I have been at all unhappy during these last few years. I probably have improved both mentally and physically and if I had been spared, might have made good in a business sense. However, now that Willie has gone, I am afraid that things will never be the same. There is only one thing that troubles me and that is the pain and trouble it will give you all at home, but I hope and trust that you will not take it too much to heart and that in time the kids will do more than Willie and I were able to do. I don't think I have much more to say and won't burden you with wishes that may be incapable of being carried out. Whatever happens, keep a good heart. With very best love to Bessie, the kiddies and yourself. I am,

> Your loving son
>
> Johnnie

Sgt John Erskine was killed at Arras in France on 14th April 1917. His name is recorded on the memorial at Arras.

Regimental Music

Regimental Band   *Within a mile of Edinburgh Toun*

Pipe Marches

Quick march 1st Bn   *Kenmuir's on an' Awa'*
Quick march 2nd Bn   *The Gathering of the Grahams*

Pipe Major and pipers, 1935

Allied and Affiliated Regiments

7th Duke of Edinburgh's Own Gurkha Rifles

Canada
The Perth Regiment

Australia
26th Battalion (The Logan and Albert Regiment)

New Zealand
The Otago and Southland Regiment

Ghana
2nd Battalion Ghana Regiment of Infantry

South Africa
The Witwatersrand Rifles

The Black Watch

Royal Highland Regiment

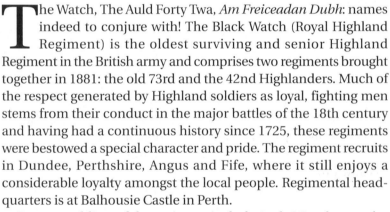

The Watch, The Auld Forty Twa, *Am Freiceadan Dubh*: names indeed to conjure with! The Black Watch (Royal Highland Regiment) is the oldest surviving and senior Highland Regiment in the British army and comprises two regiments brought together in 1881: the old 73rd and the 42nd Highlanders. Much of the respect generated by Highland soldiers as loyal, fighting men stems from their conduct in the major battles of the 18th century and having had a continuous history since 1725, these regiments were bestowed a special character and pride. The regiment recruits in Dundee, Perthshire, Angus and Fife, where it still enjoys a considerable loyalty amongst the local people. Regimental headquarters is at Balhousie Castle in Perth.

Famous soldiers of the regiment include Andy Wauchope, who was killed commanding the Highland Brigade at Magersfontein; Field Marshal Lord Wavell; General Victor Fortune, who had the painful task of overseeing the surrender at St Valery in 1940; and Brigadier James Oliver, undoubtedly the most distinguished Territorial Army Officer of recent times.

Badge

The badge of the regiment is the Star of the Order of the Thistle, upon it, the figure of St Andrew and his cross within an oval bearing the motto of the Order, *Nemo me impune lacessit* (No one provokes me with impunity). Below, the Sphinx, all ensigned with the Crown.

The badge is only worn on the Glengarry and in other forms of head-dress, only the red feather hackle is worn. This famous red hackle is the distinguishing mark of the regiment and although its origins are obscure, it is nonetheless worn with intense and jealous pride.

Regimental Origin

The Black Watch began their history in 1725, as a series of Independent Companies to 'watch' or patrol areas of the Highlands, primarily to prevent smuggling and thieving. The concept underlying such bodies was well known at that time and had been used as a security measure on several previous occasions. The Companies generally comprised groups of local and trusted men, most of whom were owners or respected tenants of land. They operated on a semi-independent

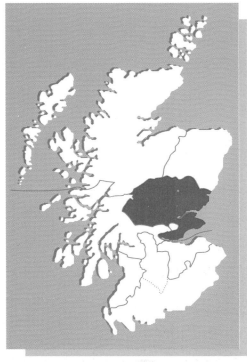

Regimental Recruiting Area

and virtually autonomous basis. In 1739, these Independent Companies were brought together to form a Highland Regiment, then numbered 43. In order to prevent ill-feeling by choosing a commanding officer from a particular clan, the command of the new Highland Regiment was given to a Lowlander, John, 20th Earl of Crawford.

Originally, the Companies appeared to have worn kilts of locally woven tartan. When the regiment was raised, however, these appeared to have been standardised into one dark tartan which became known as the Government Tartan or the Black Watch Tartan, from which many other regimental tartans originate. The name 'The Black Watch' (or in Gaelic, *Am Freiceadan Dubh*) was applied to the regiment from its earliest years. From the outset, the regiment officially wore Highland dress.

The Black Watch assembled at Aberfeldy in May 1740 and they were used in the Highlands until 1743 when they were then ordered to march to London. Many of these men had never travelled far beyond their native birthplace and were deeply suspicious of this move, fearing they were to be sent to the West Indies. An atmosphere of deep suspicion and misunderstanding existed between the Scots and other troops, largely due to differences of language and tradition and while encamped at Finchley, near London, a number of the Scots deserted and attempted to make their way back to Scotland. The Highlanders were rounded up by troops

Highland soldier, 1744

Grenadier, 1751

Officer and Private, 1856

Sergeant, 1992

of cavalry in Northamptonshire. The three ring leaders — Corporal Samuel MacPherson, Corporal Malcolm MacPherson and Private Farquhar Shaw — were executed by firing squad at the Tower of London on 18th July 1743. Of the remaining 100 or so men who survived the pursuit and trials, 26 were sent to regiments in the Mediterranean, 38 to the West Indies and 38 to Georgia.

The remaining men of the regiment embarked for Flanders and distinguished themselves with their great bravery at the Battle of Fontenoy in 1745 during the War of the Austrian Succession. In 1751, the regiment was renumbered the 42nd Regiment of Foot. In 1756, they arrived in New York to serve in actions against the French and Indians who were threatening the British colonial settlements. Led by General Abercrombie, in July 1758, they attacked the strongly fortified French position at Fort Ticonderoga. The attack was launched without artillery support and the Highlanders suffered terrible casualties. Without waiting for orders, they charged forward under murderous fire and, although commanded to retire, they only did so after losing 647 men out of their total strength of 1100.

In 1758, the regiment had been granted the title 'Royal' and a second battalion was ordered to be raised. Both the 1st and the 2nd Battalions took part in the second assault on Fort Ticonderoga which was successful. Both battalions were also present at the capture of Montreal in 1760, following which, the French lost their northern American colonies and the whole of Canada came under British control.

The regiment then served in Martinque and Havana, but in 1763, the 2nd Battalion was disbanded. After a brief spell in Ireland, the regiment returned to the New World to fight against the rebels in the War of American Independence (1776-83) at Brooklyn, Bloomingdale, Fort Washington, White Planes (1776), Brandy Wine Creek (1777) and at Yorktown (1781), after which they returned home via Canada.

In 1795, the regiment embarked for the West Indies. They then took part in the capture of Minorca (1798) and the expeditions against Genoa and Cadiz. In 1801, they were in the major assault landing at Aboukir Bay and distinguished themselves in the Battle of Alexandria, capturing the standard of Napoleon's 'Invincible Legion'. By 1808, they had joined the British army in Lisbon and they survived the retreat and evacuation at Corunna. Returning home, they took part in the ill-fated

42nd Highlander, 1758

Walcheren expedition on the Dutch coast. They returned again to Spain to fight at Salamanca, the siege of Burgos (1812) and numerous actions in the Pyrenees followed by the assault crossings of the Nivelle and the Nive. They were also present at the Battle at Toulouse (1814), where the French made a last stand.

Following Napoleon's escape from Elba, the 42nd, fighting alongside the Cameron Highlanders and the Gordon Highlanders, achieved lasting fame at Quatre-Bras and the Battle of Waterloo (1815).

After garrison service in Paris, Ireland, Gibraltar and the West Indies, The Black Watch formed part of the original force sent to the Crimea in June 1854 to join the Highland Brigade. Under the distinguished command of Sir Colin Campbell, the Brigade gained honours at the Alma and Sevastopol.

After a brief respite at home, during which the 42nd and the Highland Brigade received considerable public attention and acclaim, the regiment moved to India. There it served in the bitter fighting of the Indian Mutiny (1857-58). The campaign was conducted in the most arduous conditions of heat, dust and long marches combined with a determined and skilful enemy. Eight men of the regiment were to win the Victoria Cross at this time.

The Black Watch at the Battle of Fontenoy, 1745

The storming of Tel-El-Kebir, 1882

In 1861, the old title of The Black Watch was officially restored and the regiment became the 42nd, or the Royal Highland Regiment (The Black Watch). In 1873, it sailed for Africa's Gold Coast to take part in a extraordinary expedition against King Coffee. The expedition, known as the Ashanti Expedition, proceeded inland and entered and razed the Ashanti capital of Kumasi.

In the army reforms of 1881, the 42nd became the 1st Battalion The Black Watch (Royal Highlanders) and it was linked with the 73rd (Perthshire) Regiment which became the 2nd Battalion.

In 1779, the body of men that became the 73rd were operating as the 2nd Battalion of the 42nd Highlanders. They were raised at Perth and they were quickly sent to India to serve in the Honourable East India Company Army in Mysore. During this campaign, they defended the Great Fort at Mangalore through a long siege in 1783 with great determination and bravery. This defence earned them the nickname 'The Old Mangalore Regiment'.

In 1786, this battalion became the separate regiment called the 73rd (Highland) Regiment of Foot and in 1799, their bravery gained them the great battle honour 'Seringapatam'.

On their return to Britain in 1809, the regiment had few Scots soldiers or, indeed, Highlanders, and so lost its Highland status. After a tour of duty in New South Wales, Australia, during which the 73rd contributed a considerable amount of manual labour to the cutting of roads through the Blue Mountains, they moved to garrison duties world-wide. In 1845, they were sent to the Argentine. Afterwards, in trying and difficult conditions, they served in South Africa against the Kaffirs in the beautiful but rugged area of Eastern Cape Colony. After action in the Indian Mutiny in 1858, the 73rd returned to Great Britain to be renamed The 73rd (Perthshire) Regiment Foot.

The 73rd (Perthshire) Regiment thus had close associations with The Black Watch but, in their own right, were a proud and entirely distinctive regiment, with their own particular pattern of service and traditions. Their amalgamation to form once again a 2nd Battalion of the The Black Watch was therefore not an easy one because, during the reforms of 1881, they were essentially taken over by the 42nd and assumed the dress and traditions of The Black Watch. It is difficult to say why much of the history of this distinguished regiment was lost so rapidly, but it was widely believed at the time that the regiment had been infiltrated by members of the Fenian movement.

In 1882, the 1st Battalion (the old 42nd) distinguished itself with the Highland Brigade at the Battle of Tel El-Kabir, charging the Egyptian position with bayonets and showing great courage and determination in capturing a deep ditch and entrenchments of the enemy. The 1st Battalion then saw action in Sudan in 1884 at El Teb and at Tamaai where, in the heat of battle, men on one side of the defensive square advanced, leaving the position dangerously exposed and forcing the remainder to turn about to defend themselves. The 1st Battalion The Black Watch were

Origins of the Regiment

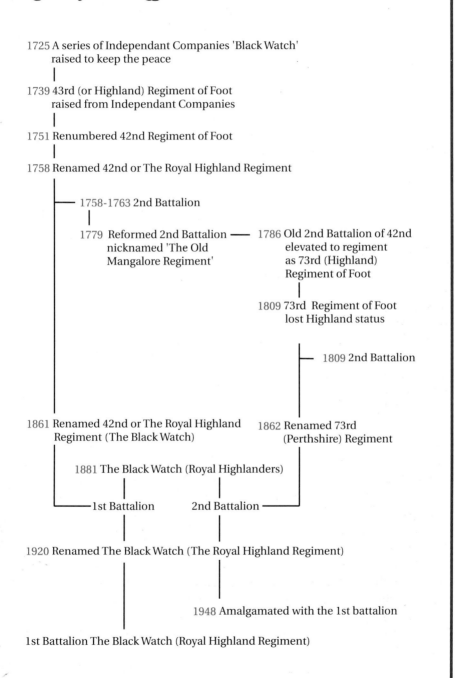

1725 A series of Independant Companies 'Black Watch' raised to keep the peace

1739 43rd (or Highland) Regiment of Foot raised from Independant Companies

1751 Renumbered 42nd Regiment of Foot

1758 Renamed 42nd or The Royal Highland Regiment

　1758-1763 2nd Battalion

　1779 Reformed 2nd Battalion — 1786 Old 2nd Battalion of 42nd
　　　　nicknamed 'The Old　　　　　elevated to regiment
　　　　Mangalore Regiment'　　　　　as 73rd (Highland)
　　　　　　　　　　　　　　　　　　　Regiment of Foot

　　　　　　　　　　　　　　　　1809 73rd Regiment of Foot
　　　　　　　　　　　　　　　　　　　lost Highland status

　　　　　　　　　　　　　　　　　　1809 2nd Battalion

1861 Renamed 42nd or The Royal Highland　1862 Renamed 73rd
　　　Regiment (The Black Watch)　　　　　　　(Perthshire) Regiment

　　1881 The Black Watch (Royal Highlanders)

　　　　1st Battalion　　　2nd Battalion

1920 Renamed The Black Watch (The Royal Highland Regiment)

　　　　　　　　　　　　1948 Amalgamated with the 1st battalion

1st Battalion The Black Watch (Royal Highland Regiment)

42nd, 73rd and Black Watch uniforms 1742–1914

also part of the force sent to relieve General Gordon at Khartoum in 1885. The regiment went on to serve in the 2nd Boer War. At Magersfontein in 1899, they were amongst the men of the Highland Brigade who were caught in open ground by a surprise Boer attack; their casualties in this one action alone numbered over 300.

At the outbreak of the First World War, the 1st Battalion The Black Watch were based in Aldershot while the 2nd Battalion was in India. Therefore, the 1st Battalion were amongst the first troops to land in France in 1914 and they took part in the early battles of Mons, Marne, Aisne and Ypres. These were desperate and difficult days. The regiment, which was brigaded in the First Infantry Brigade with The Coldstream Guards, The Scots Guards, The Royal Munster Fusiliers and The Cameron Highlanders, fought with extraordinary professional bravery and determination to prevent the German advance to the coast. At the end of these critical engagements, particularly in October and November, many of the men in these original battalions had been killed or wounded. Of those who marched from Aldershot in 1914, only 39 were still serving with the 1st Battalion The Black Watch in 1918. During the First World War, the regiment gained honours in every theatre of the Western Front as well as in Macedonia, Egypt, Gaza, Palestine, Baghdad and Mesopotamia.

On the outbreak of the Second World War, the 1st Battalion The Black Watch formed part of the 51st (Highland) Division and arrived in France in 1940. Having skilfully contributed to the retreat to Dunkirk and following the French surrender, the battalion was captured at St Valery. The 2nd Battalion served in Somaliland against the Italians. Throughout the Second World War, the men of The Black Watch distinguished themselves in the battlefields of north west Europe, North Africa, (particularly at El Alamein and at Wadi Akarit), and in Sicily, Italy, Greece, Crete and Burma.

In 1952, they joined the Commonwealth Brigade in Korea, and this was followed by action in Kenya, Cyprus and Northern Ireland.

Tartans

It is believed that the Independent Companies from which the Black Watch evolved wore their own locally woven plaid. All the indications are that these were not standard.

The 42nd Black Watch, or Government, Tartan has been worn by The Black Watch since they were first formed in 1739. The tartan is now entirely distinctive and has taken the name of the regiment. It is upon this tartan, with the application of white, red, yellow or blue strips, that many other tartans are based. Throughout the history of the Black Watch tartan, both the quality of the cloth and the size of the sett has changed considerably. Within recent memory, it was possible to distinguish between the Black Watch tartan and the tartan used by The Argyll and Sutherland Highlanders. Military standardisation, however, has meant that these two tartans are now indistinguishable. The 42nd tartan is used to make up kilts and trews in the regiment, while the pipers wear the Royal Stuart tartan.

The 73rd, in their previous incarnation as the old 2nd Battalion of the 42nd Highlanders and before 1809, also wore this same Government, or Black Watch, tartan. When the 73rd lost Highland status in 1809, they did not wear tartan again until they became the 2nd Battalion The Black Watch(Royal Highlanders) in 1881.

Black Watch tartan

Clan or Scottish Family Affiliations

The Black Watch has a wide range of clan and family affiliations. Amongst those commissioned to raise the original Independent Companies were Lord Lovat, Sir Duncan Campbell of Lochnell and Colonel Grant of Ballindalloch.

When these Companies were brought together and the 42nd was raised in 1739, John, 20th Earl of Crawford was appointed colonel. The Crawfords were a scion of the ancient Scottish Border family of Lindsay. The 73rd was first commanded by Lieutenant-Colonel Norman MacLeod and are associated with one of the most historic and romantic clans in Scotland.

In common with other Highland regiments and particularly with The Highlanders (Seaforth, Gordons and Camerons), The Black Watch still retain close family ties amongst their officers and soldiers. Many men are related to one another and even today it is not uncommon to find sons following fathers, grandfathers and uncles into the regiment.

‘Battle Honours

The battle honours of The Black Watch are an extraordinary recital of some of the greatest feats of arms of the British army in recent history. The names which adorn the colours won by the 42nd and the 73rd regiments, frequently under the most trying of conditions, are dearly coveted as part of regimental tradition and legend. Often, however, it is the case that great bravery is displayed but victory remains elusive. The withdrawal to the Battle of St Valery is such a case. It is often said that a boxer never remembers his victories, but equally never forgets his losses. More than 50 years after the event, soldiers of The Black Watch recall their part in ensuring that the evacuations of the British and French forces at Dunkirk were possible.

In March 1940, the 1st Battalion The Black Watch joined the 51st (Highland) Division in the Maginot Line, near Metz, during the 'Phoney War, the period of relative calm that followed the outbreak of war in 1939. On 10th May, the German blitzkrieg began and the Highland Division held their positions in furious fighting until they were ordered to withdraw five days later to conform to the French defence plan.

The key words for the men during this critical month were, 'march, dig-in and fight'. By the time The Black Watch reached Etian and Varennes, they learned that the French armies were disintegrating and that the Germans had broken through with an armoured attack, driving a wedge between the Highland Division and the other British formations. The Highland Division retired on Paris and, exhausted and battle weary, took up a defensive line in the area of Abbeville from whence they attacked the enemy bridgehead. A Company of the 1st Battalion The Black Watch took its objective, but the men on the flanks could not get through and the battalion had to withdraw. The 4th Battalion were also involved in this bitter fighting and they succeeded in holding off a determined German attack before the whole division was ordered to withdraw toward Dieppe. By this time, the evacuation at Dunkirk was well underway and the Highland Division, which had also hoped for evacuation, was finally cut off. The 4th Battalion were fortunate to get through to Cherbourg where they embarked for England, but the 1st Battalion fell back onto St Valery as the German armoured ring tightened. Under heavy bombardment and exhausted after a month of continuous fighting, Major General Victor Fortune surrendered at St Valery-En-Caux to General Erwin Von Rommel eight days after the evacuation of Dunkirk was complete.

At the time, many of the men of the Highland Division felt bitter and angry, but their bravery and determination and the key part which they played in allowing the evacuations to take place stands as a testimony to their courage. Of those who survived the withdrawal and rear guard actions, few escaped to fight again. The majority of the division turned their backs to the sea and marched into prisoner-of-war camps for the duration of the hostilities. After the Normandy landings in 1944, the rejuvenated 51st (Highland) Division returned St Valery in triumph.

Victoria Cross Winners

Lt F.E.H. Farquharson	42nd Highland Regiment	1858	Indian Mutiny
QMS J. Simpson	42nd Highland Regiment	1858	Indian Mutiny
Private J. Davis	42nd Highland Regiment	1858	Indian Mutiny
Private E. Spence	42nd Highland Regiment	1858	Indian Mutiny
L/Cpl A. Thompson	42nd Highland Regiment	1858	Indian Mutiny
C/Sgt W. Gardner	42nd Highland Regiment	1858	Indian Mutiny
Private W. Cook	42nd Highland Regiment	1859	Indian Mutiny
Private D. Millar	42nd Highland Regiment	1859	Indian Mutiny
L/Sgt S. McGraw	42nd Highland Regiment	1874	Ashanti
Private T. Edwards	1st Bn The Black Watch	1884	Sudan
L/Cpl D. Finlay	2nd Bn The Black Watch	1915	France
Private C. Melvin	2nd Bn The Black Watch	1917	Mesopotamia
A/Lt Col. L.P. Evans	The Black Watch (commanding 1st Bn Lincolnshire Regiment	1917	Belgium
Cpl J. Ripley	1st Bn The Black Watch	1918	France

Lt F. E. H. Farquharson V.C.

The first man to win the Victoria Cross in The Black Watch was Lieutenant Francis Edward Henry Farquharson. Farquharson was born in Glasgow on 25th March 1837. He joined the 42nd regiment and sailed with them to serve in India in 1858. Francis Farquharson was to be one of eight members of the regiment who were to win the Victoria Cross during the Mutiny. At the time, Farquharson was a young lieutenant, having been commissioned in 1855. His action took place on 9th March 1857 during the bitter fighting to recapture the city of Lucknow. He went on to be promoted to Brevet Major in 1874 and he died at Harberton, Devon, on 12th September 1875.

Regimental Pipe Music

Pipe Marches

March past in quick time   *Highland Laddie*

Company March

A Company	*Atholl Highlanders*
B Company	*Lord Alexander Kennedy*
C Company	*The Brown Haired Maiden*
D Company	*Scotland the Brave*
HQ Company	*The Road to the Isles*
Support Company	*The Steam Boat*

Crimean Reveille

The Soldiers Return
Grannie Duncan (played in slow time)
Sae Will We Yet
Grannie Duncan (played in quick time)
Miss Gridle
Chisholm Castle
Johnnie Cope

Piper, 1992

Allied and Affiliated Regiments

Canada

The Black Watch (Royal Highland Regiment) of Canada
The Lanark and Renfrew Scottish Regiment
The Prince Edward Island Regiment

Australia

The Royal New South Wales Regiment
The Royal Queensland Regiment

New Zealand

1st and 2nd Squadron New Zealand Scottish

South Africa

Transvaal Scottish

The Highlanders

Seaforth, Gordons and Camerons

On Saturday 17th September 1994 at Dreghorn Barracks on the edge of Edinburgh, an historic parade was held to amalgamate the Queen's Own Highlanders and The Gordon Highlanders. As the Colours were marched on, the newest regiment in the British Army, The Highlanders (Seaforth, Gordons and Camerons), was formed.

The amalgamation was not without opposition, not because of mutual dislike but because the people of the north, from whom these regiments traditionally draw their recruits, are proud of their military heritage and the historic part that their regiments have played in the defence of the United Kingdom. However, 'Options for Change', the plan to reduce Britain's defence forces following the break up of the Soviet Bloc, won the day and this new regiment assumes the enormous responsibility of carrying on the traditions of the Queen's Own Highlanders and The Gordon Highlanders.

Badge

On amalgamation, The Highlanders adopted the badge formerly worn by the Queen's Own Highlanders as part of the carefully woven set of compromises which are always required when the traditions of great regiments have to be merged. The badge is a stag's head caboshed, between the attires, the Thistle ensigned with the Crown, with the motto *Cuidich 'n Righ* which means 'Tribute to the King' or 'Help the King'. The Highlanders are the only regiment to have a Gaelic motto.

The origins of this motto are lost in the mists of time. Some have it that it originates from the annual feudal tribute of a stag which the MacKenzies of Seaforth were required to pay to the king each year to retain their lands in Kintail. Others attribute the motto to an incident which is reputed to have occurred when King Alexander III of Scotland was once hunting in the Forest of Mar. The king had been charged and unhorsed by an angry stag and was lying helpless on the ground. He was saved by an ancestor of the MacKenzies of Seaforth, Colin of Kintail, who killed the stag, crying out 'Cuidich 'n Righ' as he did so.

The Thistle and Imperial Crown is the badge of Scotland, approved at the time of the Act of Union in 1707 and conferred upon The Cameron Highlanders by Queen Victoria in

Regimental Recruiting Area

Formation Day parade. The Colours of the Queen's Own Highlanders (Seaforth and Camerons) and the Colours of The Gordon Highlanders march on

118

1873, when they achieved the unique distinction amongst Highland regiments of being entitled the 'Queen's Own Cameron Highlanders'. The collar badge is the Elephant with the 78th Highlander's battle honour 'Assaye', and the Tiger earned by the old 75th Highlanders in India. The waist belt plate shows the figure of St Andrew and his cross, below which is the great battle honour of both the Camerons and the Gordons, 'Waterloo'. The pipers and drummers wear a white hair sporran with two black tassels while officers and men wear black hair sporrans with two white tassels.

The blue hackle worn in the head-dress of The Highlanders originates from the time of the Second World War. The Highland regiments of the British Expeditionary Force (BEF) originally went to France wearing the kilt, their authorised uniform at this time. The War Office later ordered all active service units to wear standard battle dress blouse and trousers. This order was bitterly resented by the Highland regiments and vociferous appeals were lodged. In December 1939, King George VI, Colonel-in-Chief of the Cameron Highlanders, visited the BEF and was lobbied by the commanding officer of the 1st Battalion of the Camerons: if they were to lose the kilt, would it not be possible for some distinctive symbol, such as a white hackle, to be introduced? The king agreed but suggested that the hackles be royal blue rather than white; by February 1940, the hackles were in use. Three months later, the 1st Battalion The Queen's Own Cameron Highlanders were evacuated at Dunkirk, the last Highland battalion to have worn the kilt in action.

The royal-blue hackle was officially authorised for The Queen's Own Cameron Highlanders in 1951 and was subsequently adopted by the Queen's Own Highlanders in 1961 and by The Highlanders in 1994.

Regimental Origins

Just as The Highlanders emerged from the Queen's own Highlanders and the Gordons, these regiments were themselves the product of other amalgamations; it is thus possible to trace the origins of the Army's newest regiment back to no less than five other regiments dating from the last quarter of the 18th century

The Queen's Own Highlanders were created as a result of the amalgamation of two unique and distinguished regiments, The Seaforth Highlanders and The Queen's Own Cameron Highlanders, on the 7th February 1961. The regiment traced an unbroken history as far back as 1778 and was credited in the Army List with almost 200 battle honours. The family tree of the regiment shows the three entirely distinct roots which were bound together to form the Queen's Own Highlanders. The old regimental numbers, and more especially the names, may have changed over the years but this regiment finds its origins in the 72nd (Highland) Regiment of Foot (originally numbered 78th) raised by Kenneth, Earl of Seaforth in 1778, in the 78th (Highland) Regiment of Foot raised by Francis Humberstone MacKenzie of Seaforth in 1793 and in the 79th Regiment of Foot (or Cameron Highlanders) raised by Alan Cameron of Erracht also in 1793. In order to recruit, all of these men

Kenneth, Earl of Seaforth

Alan Cameron of Erracht

called upon traditional clan loyalties, although Alan Cameron, not a rich or powerful land owner in his own right and facing opposition from the Duke of Gordon who was trying to find recruits for the 100th Regiment, supplemented his main source of recruits in Lochaber with Highlanders drawn from other areas of Scotland where they had been forced to move in search of work.

The numbering of these regiments can be slightly confusing. It is important to remember that a regiment could be raised and given one number and then be assigned another. Thus the regiment raised by Kenneth, Earl of Seaforth in 1778 was originally given the number 78 but later renumbered as the 72nd. The regiment raised by Francis Humberstone MacKenzie in 1793 was assigned the now vacant number 78, which it kept until the old numbering system was abandoned in 1881. However, Kenneth's regiment and Francis' regiment were always two entirely separate and distinct bodies, their only connection being that they were both recruited by chiefs of the Clan Mackenzie from the traditional lands of the clan.

All of these Highland regiments in British service were run and organised against the backdrop of clan and family. Many of the men were native Gaelic speakers, many had never before left their native place and tradition, and suspicion of 'outsiders' ran deep. Such tradition and suspicion led to famous incidents, such as the renowned 'Mutiny of the Macraes'. In September 1778, the Earl of Seaforth's regiment was in Edinburgh and was ordered to move to the Channel Islands. Believing

Origins of the Regiment

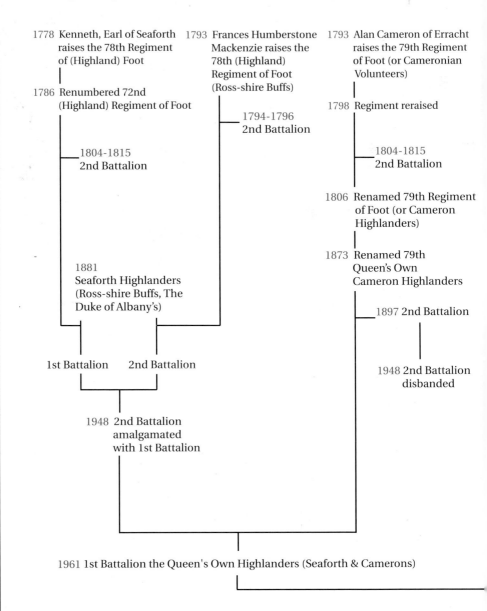

1778 Kenneth, Earl of Seaforth raises the 78th Regiment of (Highland) Foot

1786 Renumbered 72nd (Highland) Regiment of Foot

1793 Frances Humberstone Mackenzie raises the 78th (Highland) Regiment of Foot (Ross-shire Buffs)

1794-1796 2nd Battalion

1804-1815 2nd Battalion

1881 Seaforth Highlanders (Ross-shire Buffs, The Duke of Albany's)

1st Battalion   2nd Battalion

1948 2nd Battalion amalgamated with 1st Battalion

1793 Alan Cameron of Erracht raises the 79th Regiment of Foot (or Cameronian Volunteers)

1798 Regiment reraised

1804-1815 2nd Battalion

1806 Renamed 79th Regiment of Foot (or Cameron Highlanders)

1873 Renamed 79th Queen's Own Cameron Highlanders

1897 2nd Battalion

1948 2nd Battalion disbanded

1961 1st Battalion the Queen's Own Highlanders (Seaforth & Camerons)

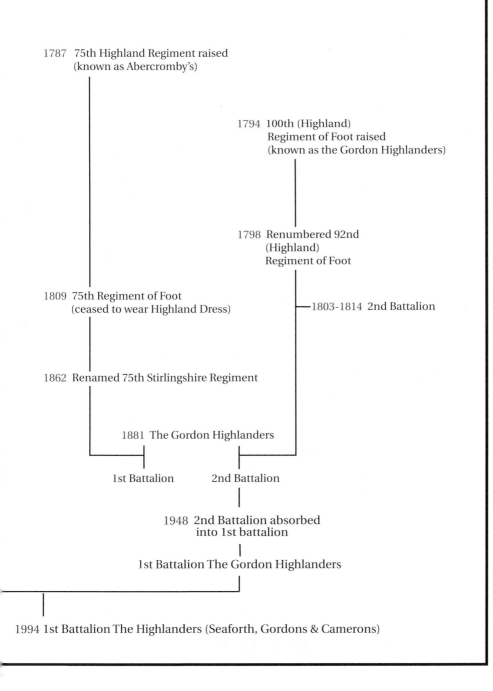

1787 75th Highland Regiment raised
(known as Abercromby's)

1794 100th (Highland)
Regiment of Foot raised
(known as the Gordon Highlanders)

1798 Renumbered 92nd
(Highland)
Regiment of Foot

1809 75th Regiment of Foot
(ceased to wear Highland Dress)

1803-1814 2nd Battalion

1862 Renamed 75th Stirlingshire Regiment

1881 The Gordon Highlanders

1st Battalion   2nd Battalion

1948 2nd Battalion absorbed
into 1st battalion

1st Battalion The Gordon Highlanders

1994 1st Battalion The Highlanders (Seaforth, Gordons & Camerons)

Soldiers of the 72nd on their return from the Crimea, 1856

themselves to have been sold to the East India Company and far from their homes and lands, the men refused to embark. A group of them led by 'the wild Macraes' from Kintail took up positions on Arthur's Seat and only after extensive negotiations was a compromise reached and the men returned to the regiment having been granted immunity from disciplinary action.

Between the time of their formation and 1881, these three great regiments, the 72nd, 78th and the 79th were fighting, serving, marching, guarding and dying both at home and in the far flung outposts of the British Empire.

By 1782, the 72nd were in India where they fought with the Honourable East India Company's army against Tipoo, Sultan of Mysore in the Carnatic Campaign. They fought alongside the 71st Highland Light Infantry and the 93rd Sutherland Highlanders to capture the Cape of Good Hope from the Dutch in 1806. They took part in two Kaffir wars, industrial riots in England and disturbances in Ireland. The regiment also fought in the Crimean War and went on to play a notable part in the Indian Mutiny. In the campaign in Afghanistan in 1878, under the command of the great General Roberts V.C., they took part in the famous march from Kabul to Kandahar.

The 78th Highlanders (Ross-shire Buffs) were on active service within a year of being raised and, under the command of Prince Frederick, Duke of York, they fought in the campaign in the Netherlands against the French Revolutionary army. The fighting was conducted in atrocious weather conditions and against a background of appaling logistics and organisation and it was from this campaign that the   nursery rhyme and dance was written:

'The Grand Old Duke of York,
He had ten thousand men.
He marched them up to the top of the hill,
and he marched them down again.'

After a sortie to Brittany to aid the French Royalists, the 78th moved to India where they distinguished themselves at the Battle of Assaye, after which they went to Java in 1811 to fight and survive for five years in one of the least known campaigns against the French. They also served overseas in India, Aden, Persia and during the Indian Mutiny; in the latter campaign, the 78th played an outstanding part in the relief of the garrison at Lucknow, and as one of the first regiments to return to Britain after the Mutiny, they were popularly acclaimed as 'The Saviours of India'.

Like the 72nd, the 78th were in Ireland, dealing with riots, in Londonderry, Belfast, Downpatrick and Ballymena and they also served in Afghanistan in 1879.

The 79th played an equally outstanding part in the nation's history. In 1794, they were with the 78th in the Netherlands, under the command of the Duke of York. When they returned to England, news came that the men of the regiment were to be drafted to other regiments which effectively meant that the 79th would cease to exist. Allan Cameron of Erracht sought an urgent meeting with the Duke of York to complain vehemently about such a proposal, saying that the king would never dare do such a thing to the 79th. 'The King, my father', replied the Duke, 'will certainly send the regiment to the West Indies'. This option was more than Allan Cameron could take and losing his temper, he stated bluntly, 'You may tell the King, your father, from me, that he may send us to Hell if he likes, and I'll go at the head of them, but he daurna draft us'.

On 10th July 1795, the 79th sailed for the West Indies. In the space of two years, yellow fever and malaria killed 267 men of the regiment. With the regiment so

QUEEN'S (
(SEAFOR

Drummer
78th (Later 72nd) Highlanders
1778

Piper
79th or Cameronian Volunteers
1794

Officer
78th Highlanders
(Ross-shire Buffs)
1793

Sergeant
Queen's Own Highlanders
1978

Private
72nd Duke of Alb
Own Highland
1825

Drummer
Queen's Own Highlanders
1978

Uniforms of the Queen's Own Highlanders 1778–1978 (Painting by Douglas N. Anderson)

HLANDERS
MERONS)

Band Corporal
78th Highlanders (Ross-shire Buffs)
1859

Officer
The Queen's Own
Cameron Highlanders
1900

Private
Seaforth Highlanders
1909

Drum Major
79th Cameron Highlanders
1852

Piper
Queen's Own Highlanders
1978

Officer
Queen's Own Highlanders
1978

The 79th Highlanders forming a Guard of Honour for Queen Victoria at the Palace of
Holyroodhouse, Edinbugh, 1852

reduced, Allan Cameron returned to Britain with the regimental cadre consisting
of the officers, non-commissioned officers and drummers, to begin recruiting again.
By 1798, the regiment was 780 strong and these men then fought in the Netherlands
(1799), Egypt (1801), at the siege of Copenhagen (1807), all through the Peninsula
campaign, and then at Quatre-Bras and at Waterloo (1815). During the Crimean
War, they served in the old Highland Brigade under Sir Colin Campbell and, thereafter, were sent to India, where after service quelling the mutiny of 1858-1859, they
remained until 1871.

In 1881, the 72nd and the 78th Highlanders came together to form the 1st and
2nd Battalions Seaforth Highlanders (Ross-shire Buffs, The Duke of Albany's) while
the Camerons had the unique but unsatisfactory distinction of being the only single
battalion regiment in the British army. It was a worrying time, with disquieting
rumours of disbandment or formation into a 3rd Battalion of the Scots Guards.
However, Queen Victoria herself personally intervened to ensure the continuity
of 'her' regiment, by insisting that a second battalion of Camerons was raised in
1897.

During the First World War, Seaforth battalions and Cameron battalions distinguished themselves in France, Belgium, Macedonia, Mesopotamia and Palestine.
Equally courageous service in Burma, North Africa, and Western Europe at the end
of the Second World War was followed by the disbandment or amalgamation of the
second battalions and eventually the successful amalgamation of the Seaforth and
Camerons to form the Queen's Own Highlanders in 1961.

The Gordon Highlanders also had their origins in the 18th century. The Gordon Highlanders comprised two entirely separate and distinctive regiments: the 75th Regiment raised in 1787 and known as Abercromby's Regiment and the 92nd Regiment, raised in 1794 as the 100th Regiment and known as The Gordon Highlanders.

The 75th Regiment was raised by Colonel Robert Abercromby of Tullibody, brother of Sir Ralph Abercromby. Mustering at Stirling, the 75th (Highland) Regiment of Foot was primarily intended for service in India. Within two years, it was in action on the Indian sub-continent during the 3rd Mysore War. In 1791, they took part in the complex and difficult siege at Seringapatam against Tippoo Sahib where they distinguished themselves against the élite 'Tiger Battalions'. At the start of the 4th Mysore War in 1799, the 75th were again engaged, later also fighting in the Madras Presidency, in Gujarat and in Bengal, where the regiment lost nearly half its number in casualties at the siege of Bhurtpore in 1805. Two years later, the 75th returned to Britain with an enviable fighting record, in recognition of which, authority was given for the regiment to bear the 'Royal Tiger' superscribed 'India' on the colours.

Once home, the regiment found themselves short of Scottish and, in particular, Highland recruits and, in 1809, they lost their Highland status and reverted to being a line regiment.

In 1834, the 75th were sent to South Africa and took part in the arduous operations against the Kaffirs. After a short spell at home, the regiment moved back to India in 1849 and on the outbreak of the Indian Mutiny in 1857, they completed an historic march of 48 miles in 38 hours from the hills near Simla to the field force

2nd Gordon Highlanders at the Battle of Mandorra, 1800

The 4th Ross-shire (Territorial) Bn Seaforth Highlanders, Neuve Chapelle, 1915 (Painting by Joseph Gr

'The 92nd Gateway', Sherpur, Kabul

headquarters at Umballa. During this period they saw action at Delhi and in the final assault on the city, the regiment distinguished itself at the More Bastion, the Kabul Gate, the Lahore Gate and the Burn Bastion. During the operations at Delhi, three Victoria Crosses were won by soldiers of the 75th. The regiment returned home in 1862 and were renamed The 75th Stirlingshire Regiment.

In 1881, despite all their efforts, the 75th, which had hitherto no connection at all with the 92nd, were converted to the 1st Battalion The Gordon Highlanders. Stationed in Malta at the time, the 75th's officers held a mock funeral and erected a tombstone upon which was written,

Here lies the poor old 75th,
but under God's protection,
they'll raise again in kilt and hose,
a glorious resurrection!
For by the transformatory power of Parliamentary laws,
we'll go to bed the 75th to be raised the ninety-twas!

On 18th June 1882, the 75th paraded, albeit awkwardly, in Highland uniform for the first time since 1809.

The 92nd Highland Regiment, more popularly known as The Gordon Highlanders, was raised by the 4th Duke of Gordon in 1794, largely from men from his own estate. Not all of them were willing recruits and there were often men who were encouraged by promises of rewards, bounties or security of tenure. The regiment was originally raised as the 100th Regiment and it only changed its number to 92nd in 1798. The Gordon Highlanders did not see service until 1799 when, under the young Marquess of Huntly, they joined Sir Ralph Abercromby's expedition for the campaign in Holland. A year later they sailed for Egypt and took part in the

Orders of dress, The Gordon Highlanders

Battle of Mandorra against the French, being one of only two regiments (both of which are Scottish) to have this special battle honour. The 92nd were also in action at Aboukir and Alexandria (1801) where they gained the distinction of being entitled to wear the badge of the Sphinx superscribed with the legend 'Egypt'.

In 1807, the Gordons sailed with an expedition to Copenhagen to demand the surrender of the Danish fleet. Subsequently, the regiment served under Sir John Moore during his historic retreat to Corunna. In commemoration of the defence of Corunna and the death of their commander on the battlefield, the Gordons wear black threads in their shoulder cords and black buttons on their spats.

After suffering in the disastrous Walcheren expedition to Antwerp in 1809, the Gordons returned to Spain. There the regiment gained a distinguished reputation in battle and the battle honours 'Fuentes de Onoro', 'Almaraz', 'Vittorio', 'Pyrenees', 'Nive', 'Orthes', and 'Peninsula'. Following Napoleon's return from exile, the regiment was prominent at the battles of Quatre-Bras and Waterloo, where the Gordons, with only about 300 men, charged a column of over 3,000 Frenchman.

During the Crimean War (1853-56), several hundred men from the 92nd Gordon Highlanders volunteered for other regiments but the Gordons arrived too late in the Crimea to see action. They also did not arrive in India until 1858 and were involved in mopping up operations following the Mutiny.

After a short spell in Scotland and Ireland, the Gordons returned to India in 1868. A decade later, they were in action in Afghanistan where, under General Roberts, they crossed the frontier in 1879 and marched on Kabul; they also took part in the famous march from Kabul to Kandahar in the face of great personal hardship, appalling weather, rugged mountains and suffocating dust clouds. In 1881, the 92nd Gordon Highlanders were moved to South Africa where a small detachment of the regiment fought against the Boers at the disastrous action at Majuba.

The death of Colonel Cameron of Fassieffern, Quatre-Bras, 1815

A 92nd Highlander on a camel of the
Indian Camel Corps, 1859

Brought together in 1881, the 75th Stirlingshire Regiment became the 1st Battalion The Gordon Highlanders and the 92nd Gordon Highlanders themselves became the 2nd Battalion. This union resembled a take-over rather than a marriage since, the 75th, although a distinguished regiment in its own right, was effectively subsumed by the Gordons. Time, however, would not wait for each group to settle into its new identity. The 1st Battalion The Gordon Highlanders were in action in 1882 at the Battle of Tel-El-Kebir, and joined the desert and river column to relieve General Gordon in Khartoum in 1884. By early 1895, the 1st Gordons had returned to India and marched through the wild terrain of the North West Frontier Province to relieve the garrison at Chitral. They later joined the Tirah field force and it was during a march across some of the roughest terrain in the world that the Gordons, along with the Gurkhas, assaulted an enemy position on the heights of Dargai with Piper George Findlater, shot through both ankles, playing his comrades into action to the tune *The Cock O' the North.*

The 2nd Battalion formed part of the besieged force at Ladysmith (1899-1900) during the 2nd Boer War, while the 1st Battalion suffered severe loses with the Highland Brigade at Magersfontein.

The 1st Battalion The Gordon Highlanders were amongst the first British troops to move to France in August 1914, where they took part in the exhausting retreat from Mons. In the early hours of 27th August 1914, in the confused situation and battle weary, the battalion was caught in a furious fire fight near Clary. With the exception of the transport men and three platoons, the battalion was captured. The 21 battalions of the Gordon Highlanders raised during the First World War went on to distinguish themselves in all the major battlefields in France and Belgium. Later in the war, the 2nd Battalion fought in Italy against the Austrians.

On the outbreak of the Second World War in 1939, the 1st Battalion returned to France as part of the 1st Division. In March 1940, it joined the famous 51st (Highland) Division. Covering the retreat on Dunkirk, the battalion fought desperate rear guard actions until their final surrender at St Valery on 12th of June. A similar fate also befell the 2nd Battalion The Gordon Highlanders in Singapore in early 1942 after the Japanese overran Malaysia.

Both battalions were reconstituted. The 1st Battalion was formed at Aberdeen in June 1940 from a nucleus of 100 soldiers at the depot, most of them former

The Gordons in action in Afghanistan, 1879

members of the 1st Battalion. The 2nd Battalion was reformed from the 11th battalion.

The 2nd Gordons took part in the Normandy landings and in the bitter fighting around Caen. The 1st Gordons were engaged in the landings in Italy and also on the Normandy beach-heads.

In July 1948, the Gordons were reduced in strength, the 2nd Battalion being absorbed into the 1st at this time, in common with all regular army infantry regiments except the Guards. In 1951, they moved to Malaysia, fighting terrorists in humid and difficult jungle conditions. In 1955, they saw action again during the emergency in Cyprus.

Tartans

Echoing the history of the regiment, The Highlanders wear three tartans: the MacKenzie of Seaforth tartan, the 79th or Cameron of Erracht tartan and the Gordon tartan.

The MacKenzie is based upon the Government, or Black Watch, tartan with two white stripes and one red stripe added to the sett. This tartan was also known as the 'Ross-shire military tartan' and the civilian Clan MacKenzie tartan is derived from it.

The 79th, or Cameron of Erracht, tartan was designed by Mrs Marjory Cameron of Erracht, mother of Alan Cameron of Erracht who raised the regiment. It is unique amongst the old regimental tartans in that it is not derived from the Government or Black Watch tartan.

The 79th tartan was thus a source of jealously guarded pride to the Queen's Own Highlanders and particularly to the Cameron branch of the regimental family. In 1881, when the linking of battalions was taking place, the War Office considered linking the 42nd Royal Highlanders with the 79th Queen's Own Cameron Highlanders. The problem was that both regiments would have had to wear the same tartan and obviously the 42nd had precedence. The Camerons were asked by telegram, 'Will your regiment adopt tartan of 42nd Regiment?' Risking disbandment or amalgamation, the curt reply in the negative left the War Office in no doubt that no one interferes with the 79th tartan.

Over the years, the three regiments which comprised the Queen's Own Highlanders wore several other tartans. The 72nd, Kenneth, Earl of Seaforth's regiment, originally wore the 42nd or Black Watch tartan. In 1809, the 72nd lost Highland status and became an ordinary line regiment ceasing to wear Highland dress. When, in 1823, their Highland status was restored, they wore trews, then as much the mark of a Highland man as the kilt, of Royal Stewart tartan (Prince Charles Edward Stuart sett).

The Royal Stewart tartan was also worn in its early days by the military band of the 78th, Francis Humberstone MacKenzie's regiment, and the same tartan was

MacKenzie of Seaforth tartan   Cameron of Erracht tartan

Gordon tartan

permitted to be worn by the pipers of the Camerons as a special honour conferred by King George VI in 1943 to mark the 150th anniversary of the raising of the regiment.

The colour of the facings, the material on the inside of the collars and cuffs of the jackets, were just as much a distinguishing feature in the confusion of battle as the regimental numbers or tartan. When all British infantry regiments wore red jackets, the collars and cuffs were turned back to show the regimental facing colour. In time, this facing colour was applied to the outside of the jackets, on the collars, the epaulettes, the cuffs and behind the badges of rank. The facing colour was also used as the background for the Regimental Colour and the drums.

The 72nd, Kenneth, Earl of Seaforth's regiment, wore yellow facings, while the buff facings of the 78th, Francis Humberstone MacKenzie's regiment, gave them their nickname of the 'Ross-shire Buffs'. When the two Seaforth regiments were brought together in 1881, they wore yellow until 1899, but then reverted to the coveted buff facing colour of the 78th.

The 79th Cameron Highlanders originally wore green, but when in 1873 they became the 'Queen's Own', and thus a Royal regiment, they changed to royal blue. In 1961, when the Queen's Own Highlanders were formed, they took the somewhat unusual decision to maintain not only two regimental tartans, but also two facing colours, the buff and the royal blue.

The distinctive tartan of The Gordon Highlanders was the Government tartan with a yellow stripe, which was commonly known as the Gordon Tartan. It was not a clan tartan, but was designed for the Gordon Fencibles by William Forsyth, a tartan manufacturer in Aberdeen, who commented on his innovation, 'I imagine the yellow strips will appear very lively'.

It is believed that the 75th originally wore the Government Tartan. After losing their Highland status in 1809, the 75th Regiment did not wear tartan again until 1881.

In 1994, the Amalgamation Committee of The Highlanders explained how the compromises were reached with regard to which tartan was to take prominence:

The three main tartans of the QO HLDRS and GORDONS are the:

> 78th Mackenzie of Seaforth
>
> 79th Cameron of Erracht
>
> 92nd Gordon

Such is the fundamental importance of these old military tartans in the regiments and their regimental areas, it was decided that they must all be perpetuated in the new regiment. The arrangement proposed allows every member of The Highlanders to wear all three tartans as part of his uniform.

The primacy of the QO HLDRS badge has been balanced by giving equivalent prominence to the Gordon (or 92nd) tartan. It is thus proposed that the regiment, less pipers and drummers, should wear the Gordon tartan kilt and a patch of Cameron tartan in the Balmoral bonnet; the pipers and drummers should wear the Cameron kilt and a patch of Gordon tartan in the Balmoral bonnet; and that the whole regiment should wear trews of the Mackenzie tartan.

Clan or Scottish Family Affiliations

The Highlanders are associated with several famous Scottish family names. The Queen's Own Highlanders had historic links with Clan MacKenzie and Clan Cameron. The MacKenzies are an ancient family whose lands stretched from Aird to Kintail and later included the Isle of Lewis. In 1623, Colin, the chief of the clan was created 1st Earl of Seaforth. The MacKenzies supported the Jacobite cause in the rebellion of 1715, for which they paid a heavy price, forfeiting their estates. In 1741, the Seaforth family bought back their lands and in the '45 Rising, they remained neutral.

By 1771, however, with many Seaforth lands destitute and clansmen hungry, Kenneth, Earl of Seaforth offered to raise a regiment for service to the Crown, in an attempt to provide employment and income for his tenants. This offer was finally accepted in 1778 and the men of the 72nd Regiment were recruited almost entirely from MacKenzie lands.

Francis Humberstone MacKenzie, Kenneth's cousin and eventual successor to the Seaforth title and chieftainship of the Clan MacKenzie, applied to raise his own regiment from clan lands in 1793. The 78th Highlanders were recruited mainly from the Seaforth estates in Ross-shire and Lewis and so both the 72nd and the 78th had almost identical clan and family associations, a link which has remained strong ever since.

The Camerons of Erracht were descended from the Lochiel chiefs of Clan Cameron. Having fought for the Jacobites in 1745, most of the clan leadership escaped to exile or were imprisoned. The Camerons were one of the few prominent families left in Lochaber during the bleak period of military rule after the '45 and Alan Cameron emerged as a popular and respected local figure during this time. On the outbreak of war with France in 1793, more troops were urgently needed and Alan's application to raise a Clan Cameron regiment was approved. By a strenuous recruiting campaign in Lochaber and throughout Scotland, he achieved his aim of raising the 79th Cameron Volunteers as a regiment of the Clan Cameron. This close association between clan and regiment has remained a strong feature for over 200 years.

The Gordon Highlanders were associated with the family of Robert Abercromby of Tullibody, brother of Sir Ralph Abercromby who raised the 75th Regiment in 1787. The 92nd Gordon Highlanders were linked with the great house and clan of Gordon.

The name Gordon is derived from the parish of Gordon in Berwickshire. The family originates from Anglo-Normans who settled in the south of Scotland in the 12th century. In the reign of Robert the Bruce (1306-29), Sir Adam, Lord of Gordon obtained a grant of the lordship of Strathbogie in Aberdeenshire. It was the 4th Duke of Gordon and his wife, Jean Maxwell, who raised The Gordon Highlanders primarily on their estates in the north east. So powerful was the Clan Gordon in the Highlands that the chief was nicknamed 'The Cock of the North'. On the death of the 5th Duke of Gordon, the title became extinct and George, 5th Earl of Aboyne succeeded as 9th Marquess of Huntly and Chief of the Clan. The once-magnificent family seat at Huntly Castle now lies in ruins.

Battle Honours

On their formation, The Highlanders fell heir to a highly impressive array of battle honours from its parent regiments, each one in its own right representing endeavour, perseverance, loyalty and courage of the highest order. The following examples are ample demonstration of these qualities.

Of the many battle honours of the 79th Cameron Highlanders, probably the best known is 'Waterloo'. The 79th arrived on the field of battle on a wet and humid day on 17th June 1815, having fought for the best part of the previous day through the hedges, ditches and cornfields of Quatre-Bras, where they had lost almost half of their fighting strength dead and wounded. A miserable night in the fields saw the weather improve slightly on the morning of the 18th when the Camerons were placed at the centre of the Allied line, just to the east of the main Brussels-Charleroi road. The morning air was cut by the sound of muskets being fired off to dry them out and the cheers of the French as Napoleon rode through his army to encourage his men. The Camerons were first involved in the battle in the early afternoon. Moving forward out of the sunken road through a hedge, they engaged the French with a heavy and effective volley of fire followed by a bayonet charge. The enemy infantry retreated down the slope, pursued by British cavalry. The French cavalry, however, then launched a determined attack and the 79th formed a defensive square. As the French attacked, Piper Kenneth MacKay, weary, mud-stained but showing no fear, moved outside the protection of the square and began playing the traditional rallying tune, *Cogadh no Sith* (War or Peace - The True Gathering of the Clans). Piper MacKay's personal and individual courage undoubtedly subscribed to the 79th Cameron Highlanders being one of only four regiments specifically mentioned by the Duke of Wellington in his Waterloo despatch. For his bravery, Kenneth Mackay was presented with a set of silver mounted pipes by the king.

Probably one of the greatest feats of arms amongst many undertaken by the Gordons was the march under the command of General Sir Frederick Roberts of the Column from Kabul to the relief of Kandahar during the Afghan War. The force had crossed the frontier in 1879 and had achieved success in the actions at Charasia and at Sherpur near Kabul, where The Gordon Highlanders distinguished themselves. In July 1880, the 2nd British Field Force based at Kandahar suffered an appalling defeat at Maiwand (1881).

Piper Kenneth Mackay at Waterloo, 1815

On 3rd August on the instructions of the viceroy, Roberts began his historic march to relieve the force at Kandahar. In three weeks, a force of 9900 men with 8000 fol-lowers and 8000 pack animals marched 320 miles across some of the most difficult terrain in the world. Each day, the 'rouse' sounded at 2.45 a.m. and by 4.00 a.m. the tents had been struck, the baggage packed and everybody was ready to start. Marching was constantly interrupted by exhausted men, scarcity of water, sand-storms, dust and the attentions of the Afghans who harried the column along its entire route. For most of the march, The Gordon Highlanders formed the rear guard, a frustrating and difficult business involving lengthy waits and constant attention to duty. Often the rear guard did not get into camp until long after dark. One of the greatest problems was the variation in temperatures from the extreme cold of the high passes to the tremendous suffocating heat of the unshaded plains.

On 31st August, the column arrived at Kandahar. The journey had taken twenty-one marching days with two halts. This extraordinary feat culminated in a stiff fight when the Gordons succeeded in recapturing some of the guns lost at Maiwand.

Victoria Cross Winners

Private T. Beach	92nd Gordon Highlanders	1854	Crimea
Ensign R. Wadeson	75th Regiment	1857	Indian Mutiny
Private P. Green	75th Regiment	1857	Indian Mutiny
C/Sgt C. Coghlan	75th Regiment	1857	Indian Mutiny
Lt A. C. Bogle	78th Highlanders	1857	Indian Mutiny
Lt J. P. H. Crowe	78th Highlanders	1857	Indian Mutiny
Lt H. T. MacPherson	78th Highlanders	1857	Indian Mutiny
Surgeon J. Jee	78th Highlanders	1857	Indian Mutiny
Asst Surgeon V. M. McMaster	78th Highlanders	1857	Indian Mutiny
C/Sgt S. MacPherson	78th Highlanders	1857	Indian Mutiny
Pte H. Ward	78th Highlanders	1857	Indian Mutiny
Pte J. Hollowell	78th Highlanders	1857	Indian Mutiny
Lt A. S. Cameron	72nd Duke of Albany's Own Highlanders	1858	Indian Mutiny
L/Cpl G. Sellar	72nd Duke of Albany's Own Highlanders	1879	Afghanistan
Major G. White	92nd Gordon Highlanders	1879	Afghanistan
Lt W.H. Cunyingham	92nd Gordon Highlanders	1879	Afghanistan
Private E. Lawson	1st Bn Gordon Highlanders	1897	India

Piper G. Findlater	1st Bn Gordon Highlanders	1897	India
Captain M. Meiklejohn	2nd Bn Gordon Highlanders	1899	South Africa
Sgt Maj. W. Robertson	2nd Bn Gordon Highlanders	1899	South Africa
Captain E. Towse	1st Bn Gordon Highlanders	1899/1900	South Africa
Captain W.E. Gordon	1st Bn Gordon Highlanders	1900	South Africa
Cpl J. F. Mackay	1st Bn Gordon Highlanders	1900	South Africa
Captain D.R. Younger	1st Bn Gordon Highlanders	1900	South Africa
Sgt J. MacKenzie	Seaforth Highlanders	1900	Ashanti
Sgt D. D. Farmer	1st Bn The Queen's Own Cameron Highlanders	1900	South Africa
Pte R. Tollerton	1st Bn The Queen's Own Cameron Highlanders	1914	First World War
Drummer W. Kenny	2nd Bn Gordon Highlanders	1914	Western Front
Lt. J. A. O. Brooke	2nd Bn Gordon Highlanders	1914	Western Front
Lt Col. A. F. Douglas-Hamilton	6th Bn The Queen's Own Cameron Highlanders	1915	First World War
Cpl J. D. Pollock	5th Bn The Queen's Own Cameron Highlanders	1915	First World War
Cpl S. W. Ware	1st Bn Seaforth Highlanders	1916	First World War
Dmr W. Ritchie	2nd Bn Seaforth Highlanders	1916	First World War
Capt N. G. Chavasse	1/10 (Scottish) Bn King's (Liverpool) Regiment	1916	First World War
Capt N. G. Chavasse V.C.	1/10 (Scottish) Bn King's (Liverpool) Regiment	1917	First World War
L/Sgt T. Steel	1st Bn Seaforth Highlanders	1917	First World War

Lt D. MacKintosh	2nd Bn Seaforth Highlanders	1917	First World War
Sgt A. Edwards	6th Bn Seaforth Highlanders	1917	First World War
L/Cpl R. McBeath	5th Bn Seaforth Highlanders	1917	First World War
Private G. I. McIntosh	1/6th Bn Gordon Highlanders	1917	Western Front
Sgt J. M. Meikle M.M.	4th Bn Seaforth Highlanders	1918	First World War
Lt A. E. Ker	3rd Bn Gordon Highlanders	1918	Western Front

V.C.s won by Allied Regiments

Capt T. W. MacDowell	38th Ottawa Bn CEF	1917	First World War
Lt R. Shankland	The Cameron Highlanders of Canada	1917	First World War
Private C. J. P. Nunney	38th Ottawa Bn CEF	1918	First World War
Private E. A. Smith	The Seaforth Highlanders of Canada	1944	Second World War

While the 78th Highlanders' record is remarkable in gaining eight Victoria Crosses in the space of three months during the Indian Mutiny, and more particularly in the relief of the garrison of Lucknow, the 79th Cameron Highlanders were notable in that they had no Victoria Cross winners until Sgt Donald Farmer received the award on 13th December 1900 during the South African War.

This apparent lack of attainment was not a matter of chance, but a part of regimental policy and pride. In Victorian Scotland, the 79th believed that it was a soldier's responsibility to do his duty in peace and war, that excellence was expected and that no reward should be sought for simply getting on with the job, whatever the dangers. The Camerons were not alone in taking this view as a regiment and thus the award of the Victoria Cross to Donald Farmer was all the more poignant and meaningful.

Donald Dickson Farmer who was born in Kelso, Roxburghshire, on the 28th May 1877, was one of the many Border Scots belonging to the Cameron Highlanders at the turn of the century. He joined the regiment in March 1892 and served through the Soudan Campaign of 1898, where he was present at the battles of Atbara and Khartoum. On the 13th December 1900, Sergeant Farmer, then serving with the Mounted Infantry company under the command of Lieutenant Sandilands of the Camerons, went with fifteen other men to assist a heavily attacked picquet at

General Clement's camp at Nooitgedacht. It was dawn, many of the men of the picquet were dead when the Camerons arrived and the enemy, who were hidden in trees, opened fire at a range of only 20 yards. Immediately, two Cameron Highlanders were killed and five wounded, including Lieutenant Sandilands. Sergeant Farmer immediately went to Sandiland's aid and under very heavy and accurate fire, managed to carry the officer clear. He then returned to the firing line and was eventually taken prisoner when the position was overrun. Six men of the Cameron Highlanders were killed and eleven were wounded in this disastrous action.

Donald Farmer became a Colour Sergeant in 1905. He served with the Liverpool Scottish during the First World War, where he received a Quartermaster's Commission and was appointed Adjutant. Eventually,

C/Sgt D. Farmer V.C.

he rose to the rank of Lieutenant Colonel. This remarkable soldier died in 1956, only a few months after attending a review of Victoria Cross holders by Her Majesty Queen Elizabeth II.

Probably the most famous Victoria Cross awarded to a Gordon Highlander is that of Piper, later Pipe Major, George Findlater. Findlater was born at Forgue, Huntly, Aberdeenshire in 1872. He joined the 1st Battalion The Gordon Highlanders and in 1897, he was in India when the Tirah expeditionary force was formed to quell the rebellious Afridi and Orakzai tribes. Marching from Peshawar, the column moved through the Kohat pass to the lower slopes of the Samana range of mountains. A series of brief and frequently bloody exchanges culminated in an attack on a hilltop position over narrow and exposed ground near the village of Dargai. Large numbers of the enemy occupied the high ground in defensive positions. Their resistance was determined and their fire was accurate. The 2nd Gurkhas led the first assault across the open ground, followed by the Dorsetshire Regiment but both were soon pinned down and could advance no further. The Gordon Highlanders were then called upon. Led by Lieutenant-Colonel Mathias, they pressed forward without hesitation, moving steadily upwards. Shouting, cheering, breathless and

Piper G. Findlater V.C.

determined, they took the position with a fearsome grit that was nothing short of heroic. As they advanced across the narrow open ground, Piper Findlater who had already begun playing as the attack gathered momentum, was hit in both ankles. Painfully he propped himself up against a rock and continued to play until the charge was completed. George Findlater received the Victoria Cross from Queen Victoria herself.

George Findlater, who was forced to retire as a result of his wounds, was later to cause considerable controversy. As a result of his exploits at Dargai he became a national hero. His wounds, however, made it difficult for him to work and there was considerable storm when he was invited to appear at the Alhambra Music Hall on a paid engagement only shortly after he had received his medal. The officers and pipers of the Depot at Aberdeen were forbidden to patronise his performance. As a result of the 'Findlater scandal' the pension associated with the Victoria Cross which had formerly been £10 per annum was raised to £50 at the Secretary of State's discretion. George Findlater died at Turriff, Aberdeenshire on 11th March 1942.

Regimental Pipe Music

Regimental marches   *The Cock O' The North*
                          Pibroch of Donuil Dubh

March past in quick time   *The Wee Highland Laddie*

March past in slow time   *The Highlander's Slow March*

Company marches
  A Company   *The Braemar Gathering*
  B Company   *Over the Chindwin*
  C/SP Company   *Farewell to the Creeks*
  D Company   *Heights of Cassino*
  HQ Company   *The Highland Brigade at Tel el Kebir*

Long Reveille   *Jessie Chisholm (slow time)*
                     Grannie Duncan (slow time)
                     Fingal's Wedding (slow time)

Long Reveille (contd)

> *Greenwoodside (quick time)*
> *Jessie Chisholm (strathspey)*

Retreat – march on   *The March of the Cameron Men*
> *Cock of the North*

Retreat – march   *The Kilworth Hills*

Retreat – march off   *Cabar Feidh*

Allied Regiments

Canada

The Cameron Highlanders of Ottawa
The 48th Highlanders of Canada
The Queen's Own Cameron Highlanders of Canada
The Seaforth Highlanders of Canada
The Toronto Scottish Regiment

Australia

The 5th/7th Battalion The Royal Australian Regiment
The Royal South Australia Regiment
The Royal Western Australia Regiment
The 5th/6th Battalion The Royal Victoria Regiment
The Scotch (PGC) College, Queensland

New Zealand

4th Battalion (Otago and Southland) Royal New Zealand Infantry Regiment
7th Battalion (Wellington [City of Wellington's Own] and Hawkes Bay) Royal
    New Zealand Infantry Regiment

South Africa

The Capetown Highlanders

The Argyll & Sutherland Highlanders

Princess Louise's

The Argyll and Sutherland Highlanders are perhaps one of the best known Highland regiments and the one with the most romantic associations. The regiment's history dates back to 1794 but it assumed its present form in 1881 following the amalgamation of the 91st Argyllshire Highlanders and the 93rd Sutherland Highlanders. Better known in Scotland simply as 'the Argylls', the regiment recruits today in central Scotland (in the old counties of Stirlingshire and Clackmannanshire) and in the west of Scotland in Argyll.

The Sutherland branch of the regiment is particularly famed for its part in the Battle of Balaklava (1854) during the Crimean War, while the regiment as a whole is remembered for its action in Aden in 1967 when the Crater District was reoccupied, and also for the huge public campaign mounted in 1968 to 'Save the Argylls' when it was threatened with disbandment.

Badge

The regimental badge is a circle inscribed 'Argyll and Sutherland' surrounded by a wreath of thistles. In the centre, the cypher of Princess Louise reversed and interlaced with the princess' coronet mounted above. The boar's head of the Duke of Argyll and the cat of the Duke of Sutherland lie within the circle.

The Argyll and Sutherland Highlanders have two mottos. The first is *Ne Obliviscaris* (Do not forget), the motto of the Duke of Argyll, and the second is *Sans Peur* (Fearless), the motto of the Duke of Sutherland. In both the badge and the motto of the regiment, therefore, the Argyll and Sutherland Highlanders retain a close association with their clan origins on Campbell and Sutherland lands.

The association with Princess Louise, fourth daughter of Queen Victoria, dates from 1870, when she became engaged to be married to the Marquis of Lorne, the eldest son of the Duke of Argyll, whose ancestor had raised the 91st Highlanders in 1794. In view of this, the 91st Highlanders asked to have the honour of forming the guard at St George's Chapel, Windsor, on the day of the wedding. Their request was granted and 100 picked men attended the ceremony in March 1871. Shortly after the wedding, Queen Victoria asked if she might confer some distinction upon the 91st to celebrate their part in the festivities. The regiment immediately asked to have the kilt restored to them (they wore trews at the time), but the War Office would not agree and a compromise was reached whereby the regiment was entitled 'Princess Louise's Argyllshire Highlanders' and was permitted, in addition, to bear the boar's head, the motto *Ne Obliviscaris*, Princess Louise's coronet and her cypher on their colours.

After 1881, when the 91st and the 93rd regiments became linked as the 1st and 2nd Battalions The Argyll and Sutherland Highlanders, the association with Princess Louise's wedding was carefully retained and woven into the badge of the new regiment.

Regimental Recruiting Area

HRH The Princess Louise

Regimental Origins

The Argyll and Sutherland Highlanders trace their origins to two separate and distinct regiments, the 98th (later 91st) Argyllshire Highlanders and the 93rd Sutherland Highlanders.

Sergeant, Piper and Private, 1893

Private, 1992

The Argyllshire Highlanders were raised against a background of the prospect of war against France in 1794. George III asked several substantial Highland land owners to raise regiments at this time, including the Duke of Argyll. The Duke, however, was not well enough to carry out such an exacting task and he delegated it to his kinsman, Duncan Campbell of Lochnell, who was then a captain in the First Foot Guards. Lochnell had considerable problems with recruiting. Over 1000 men were required in the space of three months and, although most of the officers were natives of Argyll, over two-thirds of the men had to be recruited from Lowland towns and from Ireland.

The 93rd Sutherland Highlanders, raised in 1799 by Major General William Wemyss, a nephew of the Earl of Sutherland, was recruited under unusual circumstances for the period. General Wemyss had been particularly successful in recruiting two fencible regiments for home defence from Sutherland estates and lands. The last of these regiments had just been disbanded when Wemyss set to

Origins of the Regiment

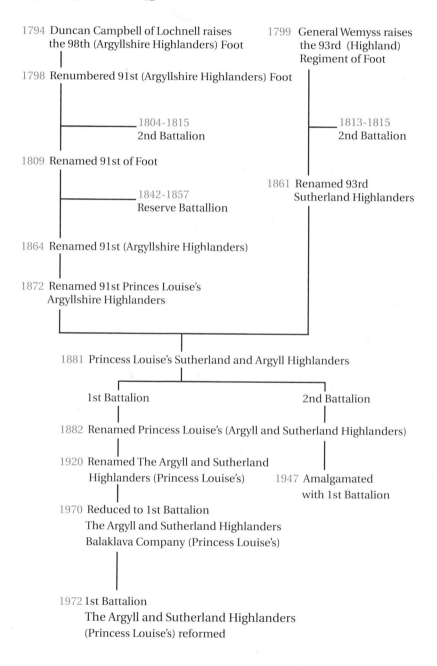

1794 Duncan Campbell of Lochnell raises the 98th (Argyllshire Highlanders) Foot

1799 General Wemyss raises the 93rd (Highland) Regiment of Foot

1798 Renumbered 91st (Argyllshire Highlanders) Foot

1804-1815 2nd Battalion

1813-1815 2nd Battalion

1809 Renamed 91st of Foot

1861 Renamed 93rd Sutherland Highlanders

1842-1857 Reserve Battallion

1864 Renamed 91st (Argyllshire Highlanders)

1872 Renamed 91st Princes Louise's Argyllshire Highlanders

1881 Princess Louise's Sutherland and Argyll Highlanders

1st Battalion

2nd Battalion

1882 Renamed Princess Louise's (Argyll and Sutherland Highlanders)

1920 Renamed The Argyll and Sutherland Highlanders (Princess Louise's)

1947 Amalgamated with 1st Battalion

1970 Reduced to 1st Battalion The Argyll and Sutherland Highlanders Balaklava Company (Princess Louise's)

1972 1st Battalion The Argyll and Sutherland Highlanders (Princess Louise's) reformed

Argylls on the Western Front, First World War

work to raise the Sutherland Highlanders. Over 250 men joined from the fencibles, while the other 390 or so were raised by levy and ballot on the Sutherland estates, where the men were actively discouraged from joining regiments other than the 93rd Sutherland Highlanders or the 78th Highlanders. In 1799 and early 1800, a census was taken of each parish on the Sutherland estates and the eligible men were summoned to appear on the open fields adjacent to the parish churches. Not all were willing to go, and not all of the parents were happy to see their sons enter the service. However, the men were drawn up and the general with an aide passed through the ranks with a snuff mill and whisky. To those who were offered snuff, the signal was given that they were required for service and the 'contract' was sealed with whisky. Only in the isolated far north did this form of enlistment take place at this time.

In the years that followed, the 91st Argyllshire Highlanders saw extensive service in the Cape of Good Hope and in the Peninsular Campaign, South Africa and the Zulu War (1879). The 93rd Sutherland Highlanders were present at the Cape of Good Hope, the Battle of New Orleans (1814), the Canadian Rebellion of 1838, and they played a distinguished part in both the Crimean War (1853-56) and the Indian Mutiny (1857-58).

In 1881, these two historic regiments, which hitherto had no association, were linked to form the 1st and 2nd Battalions The Argyll and Sutherland Highlanders. The two battalions served and fought in India and South Africa. During the First World War, the regiment, with its Territorial and Service battalions, was present on the battlefields in France, Belgium and Salonica and engaged in some of the fiercest fighting. Six members of the regiment won the Victoria Cross.

During the Second World War, the Argylls served in the battle for France and the retreat to St Valery (1940) as well as in the Western Desert, Crete, Sicily and north west Europe. The 2nd Battalion, which carried on the traditions of the old 93rd Sutherland Highlanders were in Malaya at the time of the Japanese advance on Singapore in 1941. After a grim, difficult and courageous fighting retreat, the remnants of the battalion were marched into captivity. By order of the king, the 15th Battalion The Argyll and Sutherland Highlanders, then a new battalion training in England, assumed the weighty responsibility of the name, battle honours and traditions of the 2nd Battalion and the old 93rd.

After the Second World War, there followed an extremely difficulty period of service for the Argylls in Palestine, outstanding conduct in Korea and arduous duty in Suez, Cyprus, Borneo and Aden. In 1968, news was received of the proposed disbandment of the Argylls. After a huge popular campaign which achieved world-wide support, the regiment survived but was reduced to company strength. In 1971, the 1st Battalion was reborn, inheriting the traditions of the two great regiments, the 91st Argyllshire Highlanders and the 93rd Sutherland Highlanders.

Arms find, Aden, 1967

The re-entry into Crater district, Aden, 1967

Tartans

When the 91st Argyllshire Highlanders were raised, they were a kilted regiment and wore the Government, or Black Watch, tartan. The 93rd Sutherland Highlanders also wore kilts of the same tartan, which in official records is also sometimes referred to as the Sutherland tartan. This tartan is worn today by the 1st Battalion The Argyll and Sutherland Highlanders. The pipers, drummers and military bandsmen also wear the same sett.

Until relatively recently, the version of the Government tartan worn by the Argylls was of a slightly lighter shade than worn by other regiments and was clearly distinguishable, as is the elaborate silk ribboned panel on the front flap of the kilt worn by officers and senior non-commissioned officers.

Government tartan

Between 1809 and 1864, the 91st Argyllshire Highlanders lost Highland status. Ceasing to wear the kilt, or indeed any tartan at all, they wore the ordinary uniform of regiments of the line. Several attempts were made by their persistent and charismatic commanding officer, Lieutenant-Colonel Bertie Gordon, to restore tartan to the 91st and in 1864, that request was granted. There then followed a considerable debate about what constituted the original tartan of the regiment. The 91st were in India at the time, and there seemed to be no record and no one could remember with any degree of clarity. However, with the help of the Duke of Argyll, the regiment adopted and were permitted to wear Campbell of Cawdor tartan trews, being the Government tartan with a red and light blue stripe, which they wore until 1881.

For the Argylls of today, as distinctive as the regimental tartan is the 'swinging six', the six-tassled sporran, and the badger head sporrans worn by the officers and sergeants.

Clan or Scottish Family Affiliations

The Argyll and Sutherland Highlanders have direct clan affiliations to the dukes whose names they bear. While the 91st Argyllshire Highlanders may have recruited a sizeable number of their men from Lowland towns, many of these men were undoubtedly of Highland origin, forced south in search of work. The Campbells were and still are a strong and powerful clan with a history of loyalty to Government service. At the time the regiment was raised in 1794, seventeen of the officers bore the name Campbell and distinguishing one Campbell from another posed problems. Repetition of Christian names also created difficulties. Four officers had the name 'Archibald', three 'Duncan', three 'James', two 'John' and two 'Colin'. The problem was a common feature of Highland regiments, so the War Office resorted to numbering officers sequentially to differentiate them in the Army lists.

The Sutherland Highlanders were raised for service with the British army under unique circumstances. There was a deliberate attempt to raise an 'estate' regiment rather than a clan regiment from Sutherland lands. For some considerable period into the 1830s, the Sutherland connection was maintained in strength, despite the ruthless Clearances. Many of the men were also recruited from Fife, where General Wemyss had estates. It was, however, the formal loss to the regiment of the Sutherland recruiting area in 1872 that was deeply resented by the 93rd and, despite various attempts, it was never restored to them.

Battle Honours

Outstanding, unusual and unique are all words which can be applied to the many battle honours of this distinguished regiment. Two particular honours stand apart, however: 'Balaklava' and 'Malaya 1941-42'. Indeed, The Argyll and Sutherland Highlanders are the only regiment of infantry in the British army to be awarded the honour 'Balaklava'.

The 93rd Sutherland Highlanders had fought with great courage at the Battle of the Alma in September 1854 as part of Sir Colin Campbell's Highland Brigade. In October, however, the 93rd were left behind in the port of Balaklava to unload stores, while the main part of the army moved to Sevastopol to besiege the town. It is easy to imagine how cheated and dejected the regiment felt about being denied, or so it seemed, a part in the fighting.

After were several false alarms, and then with little warning, the Russians attacked and occupied the forts and outposts protecting Balaklava, the Turks defending these positions having fled. The 93rd were already under arms and in position and Sir Colin took his meagre force of cavalry, marines and Highlanders and immediately set up a defence. 'Remember there is no retreat. You must die where you stand,' he told them. As the Russian cavalry advanced, the 93rd, in line and only two deep, moved over the crest of a hill. For a long moment, all was eerily silent. The movement of the horses, the clinking of the sabres, the champing of bits could clearly be heard. No one spoke. The Russian cavalry then charged head-long toward the slender British line and, side-by-side, the Highlanders stood firm and faced the approaching onslaught.

At 600 yards, they fired a volley into the enemy cavalry which had virtually no impact on its momentum. In the face of increasing volley fire and with the Highlanders' line still unyielding, at 200 yards the leading cavalry finally began to break and wheeled to the left. The 93rd moved their defensive position in response and still stood their ground. The Russians, baulked by the Highlanders' determination, abandoned their attack and withdrew. As they retreated across the plain pursued by artillery fire, the 93rd threw their bonnets in the air and cheered. 'We expected to have to fight soldiers,' one of the Russian cavalrymen commented subsequently, 'not red devils.'

The 93rd in Crimea, 1854

Over 80 years later, in 1941, the 2nd Battalion The Argyll and Sutherland Highlanders were in Malaya when war with Japan broke out. Stationed over 300 miles north of Singapore on the Thai border, their task was to provide the rearguard to the withdrawals. Outnumbered and ill-equipped, they fought with outstanding determination. In January 1942 at Slim River, the regiment was so depleted by a Japanese tank attack that only scattered groups survived. Several of these groups fought on in isolation in the jungle. The remainder, with only three officers and 90 soldiers under Captain Tom Slessor, began the withdrawal to Singapore. After a return to and reinforcement in Singapore, this group was joined by courageous Chinese volunteers and a party of Royal Marines who were survivors of the battleships HMS *Prince of Wales* and HMS *Repulse*. This fighting combination quickly gained the nickname the 'Plymouth Argylls'. With the pipers playing *A Hundred Pipers* and *Highland Laddie*, the Argylls eventually crossed to Singapore Island and the causeway was blown.

Two weeks later, the few survivors were taken prisoner and the heroic 2nd Battalion The Argyll and Sutherland Highlanders ceased to exist. Isolated groups fought on in the jungle until they were captured. However, two men, Private Stewart and Private Bennett, remained at liberty for four years, until the return of British forces to Malaya.

Victoria Cross Winners

Capt. W.G.D. Stewart	93rd Highlanders	1857	India
C/Sgt J. Munro	93rd Sutherland Highlanders	1857	India
Sgt J. Paton	93rd Sutherland Highlanders	1857	India
L/Cpl J. Dunley	93rd Sutherland Highlanders	1857	India
Private P. Grant	93rd Sutherland Highlanders	1857	India
Private D. MacKay	93rd Sutherland Highlanders	1857	India
Lt W. McBean	93rd Sutherland Highlanders	1858	India
Capt J.A. Liddell	3rd Bn Argyll and Sutherland Highlanders & Royal Flying Corps	1915	Belgium
Lt J.R.N. Graham	9th Bn Argyll and Sutherland Highlanders	1917	Meso- potamia
2nd Lt A. Henderson M.C.	4th Bn Argyll and Sutherland Highlanders	1917	France
2nd Lt J.C. Buchan	7th Bn Argyll and Sutherland Highlanders	1918	France
Temp Lt D.L. MacIntyre	Argyll and Sutherland Highlanders	1918	France
Lieutenant W.D. Bissett	1/6 Bn Argyll and Sutherland Highlanders	1918	France
Lt-Col. L.M. Campbell D.S.O.,T.D.	7th Bn Argyll and Sutherland Highlanders	1943	N. Africa
Major J.T. McK.Anderson D.S.O.	8th Bn Argyll and Sutherland Highlanders	1943	N. Africa
Major K. Muir	1st Bn Argyll and Sutherland Highlanders	1950	Korea

The Argyll and Sutherland Highlanders are proud to claim 16 Victoria Cross winners in their history from men of the 93rd at Lucknow in 1857 to Captain J A Liddell of the Argylls, and from the Royal Flying Corps in France in 1915 to Lieutenant-Colonel Lorne Campbell at Wadi Akarit, North Africa in 1943. Taking but one of these Victoria Crosses, the outstanding courage of Major Kenneth Muir of the 1st battalion in Korea in 1950 is a complete example of the stubborn determination which The Argyll and Sutherland Highlanders have shown in battle since 1794.

Major K. Muir V.C.

Kenneth Muir was born in Chester in 1912. In 1950, he was second in command of the 1st Battalion The Argyll and Sutherland Highlanders at Songju, 100 miles north of Pusan in Korea. The Argylls, along with the 1st Battalion The Middlesex Regiment, were the first British representatives in the United Nations force at that time. The battalion had been in Korea for just one month when they advanced with The Middlesex Regiment in support of a breakout by the United States 24th Infantry Division. The occupation of high points and the protection of the flanks were crucial. The hills were numbered for reference purposes according to their height. The Middlesex Regiment successfully occupied Hill 325, and two companies of the Argylls advanced on the adjacent Hill 282, which they occupied.

The North Koreans immediately began a counter attack and, as the shelling and mortar fire increased, the Argylls' casualties mounted. Evacuating the wounded was almost impossible and extra stretcher bearers were called for. Major Muir reached Hill 282 in charge of these stretcher bearers and at once began to co-ordinate the evacuation of the wounded despite increased mortar fire. In the desperate and confused situation, with ammunition running low, artillery support was withdrawn by the US 24th Infantry Division without warning. An air strike by the United States Air Force on the enemy position was called in and the air recognition panels were laid out by the Argylls on Hill 282. The aircraft arrived overhead, circled three times, and then to everyone's horror laid napalm and machine-gun fire on the wrong hill. Hill 282 and the Argylls' position was transformed into a blazing inferno. As the air attack came in for the second time, Major Muir, having withdrawn from the hilltop, stood in full view of the enemy, waving an air recognition panel, but to no avail. Only five officers and 35 soldiers of the Argylls survived. Tirelessly, Major Muir inspired his men by his personal example, leading the fight to retake the crest of Hill 282, until he, too, was mortally wounded. By then, the only course was a fighting withdrawal. As they watched with mounting frustration, men of The Middlesex Regiment who supported this withdrawal with machine-gun fire had to be physically restrained from going up Hill 282 to help their Argyll comrades.

In war, mistakes can happen so easily and on 23rd September 1950, when challenged by a combination of events, Major Kenneth Muir displayed courage far above that which could have been expected from any man in the circumstances. He was posthumously awarded both the Victoria Cross and the American Distinguished Service Cross.

Regimental Toast

Slainte do'n Bhan Righ, slainte dhuibh uile gu leir ('Health to the Queen, health to you altogether.')

Regimental Pipe Music

March past in quick time	Highland Laddie The Campbells are Coming
The Charge	Monymusk
Company Marches	Company marches change at the discretion of the Commanding Officer.
Funerals	Lochaber No More

Both the 91st Argyllshire Highlanders and the 93rd Sutherland Highlanders have always had a rich musical tradition.

Both battalions had pipers from the very first. Although they lost Highland status in 1809, the 91st still continued to put men on parade with pipes, although in 1850, at Dover, an inspecting officer ordered them off. Ten years later, however, in India, the commanding officer, Lieutenant-Colonel Bertie Gordon was pleased to report that the captains of the companies had, at their own expense, sent to Scotland for three sets of pipes. In 1864, when the 91st adopted the title 'Argyllshire Highlanders', pipers again appeared officially and the 91st were able to boast a fine group of pipers, a fife and drum band and a military band. The fifes and drums paraded with the regiment at least until 1881 when a combination of circumstances led to their demise and the pipe band came to the fore.

As regards the military band, the Argylls were fortunate enough at the turn of the century to have one of the most distinguished and able band masters in the British army, Band Master Ricketts who, under the name of Kenneth Alford, composed a number of famous marches, including *The Thin Red Line, Colonel Bogey* and *The Great Little Army.*

Allied and Affiliated Regiments

A close association is maintained with the Royal Marines.

Canada

The Argyll and Sutherland Highlanders of Canada (Princess Louise's)
The Calgary Highlanders

Australia

The Royal New South Wales Regiment

Pakistan

1st Battalion (Scinde) The Frontier Force Regiment

Appendix 1

Battle honours of the Scottish Regiments

In 1956, the Army Council defined a battle honour as 'a public commemoration of a battle, action or engagement of which not only past and present, but also future generations of the regiment can be proud'. Today, it is generally imagined that this system of battle honours is of great antiquity and tradition, but this is not the case. In the 18th century recognition of a regiment's distinction in battle with an honour, badge, name, or motto, was entirely random and was sparingly used. The first time that an honour was ordered to be emblazoned on a regimental colour was in 1784, when four regiments were awarded the distinction 'Gibralter'.

By the time of the army re-organisation of 1881 and the amalgamation of infantry regiments, the 'system' of battle honours that had developed had little logic to it, although the honours that had been awarded were jealously guarded and proudly carried by the recipients. That year, a Committee of Enquiry under General Alison sought to establish firm guidelines for the award of battle honours. In outline, it recommended that only victories should be awarded and that to qualify the Headquarters and at least half of the strength of the regiment must have been present. At a further Committee in 1909, under General Ewart of The Queen's Own Cameron Highlanders, bold attempts were made to rationalise claims and to review anomalies again. However, it was the First and Second World Wars which transformed the regulations regarding the award and emblazoning upon colours of battle honours.

In 1922 and 1956 respectively, it was decided that up to ten honours only for each of the First and Second World Wars were permitted to be emblazoned upon the King's or Queen's colour of a regiment; these ten honours were to be printed in bold type in the army lists, as they are so indicated in the lists which follow. Individual engagements and battles were awarded, such as El Alamein, together with theatre honours, such as North West Europe 1944-45, and for the first time and quite rightly so, names such as 'Dunkirk 1940, Norway 1940 and Arnhem 1945' also appeared.

In recent times the amalgamation of various regiments had caused great difficulties in the selection of battle honours to appear on the new colour. Generally, it is agreed that those honours common to the amalgamating regiments are adopted automatically and of the remainder, it is a question of long hours of delicate discussion and negotiations.

The Royal Scots Dragoon Guards
(Carabiniers and Greys)

Blenheim
Ramillies
Oudenarde
Malplaquet
Dettingen
Warburg
Beaumont
Willems

Waterloo
Talavera
Albuhera
Vittoria
Peninsula
Balaklava
Sevastopol
Delhi 1857

Abyssinia
Afghanistan 1879–80
Relief of Kimberley
Paardeberg
S. Africa 1899–1902
Gulf 1991

The Great War

Mons
Le Cateau
Retreat from Mons
Marne 1914
Aisne 1914
Messines 1914
Armentieres 1914
Ypres 1914, 15
Nonne Bosschen
Gheluvelt
Neuve Chapelle
St Julien

Frezenberg
Bellewaarde
Loos
Arras 1917
Scarpe 1917
Cambrai 1917, 18
Lys
Hazebrouck
Somme 1918
St Quentin Avre
Amiens
Albert 1918

Bapaume
Hindenburg line
Canal du Nord
St Quentin Canal
Beaurevoir
Selle
Sambre
Pursuit to Mons
France and Flanders
   1914–18

The Second World War 1939–45 and after

Caen
Hill 112
Falaise
Venlo Pocket
Hochwald Aller
Bremen
North–West Europe
   1944–45
Merjayun
Syria 1941
Alam el Halfa
El Alamein

El Aghelia
Nofilia
Advance on Tripoli
N. Africa 1942–43
Salerno
Battipaglia
Volturno Crossing
Italy 1943
Imphal
Tamu Road
Nunshigum
Bishenpur

Kanglatongbi
Kennedy Peak
Shwebo
Sagaing
Mandalay
Ava
Irrawaddy
Yenangyaung 1945
Burma 1944–45

Gulf 1991

Scots Guards

Namur 1695
Dettigen 1743
Lincelles 1793
Talavera 1809
Barrosa 1811
Fuentes d'Onor 1811

Salamanca 1812
Nive 1813
Peninsula 1803-14
Waterloo 1815
Alma 1854
Inkerman 1854

Sevastopol 1854-56
Tel–el–Kebir 1882
Egypt 1882
Suakin 1885
Modder River 1899
S. Africa 1889–1902

The Great War (3 Battalions)

Retreat from Mons
Marne 1914
Aisne 1914
Ypres 1914, 17
Langemarck 1914
Gheluvelt 1914
Nonne Bosschen 1914
Givenchy 1914
Neuve Chapelle 1915
Aubers 1915
Festubert 1915

Loos 1915
Somme 1916, 18
Flers–Courcelette 1916
Morval 1916
Pilckem 1917
Poelcappelle 1917
Passchendaele 1917
Cambrai 1917, 18
St Quentin
Albert 1918
Bapaume 1918

Arras 1918
Drocourt–Queant
Hindenburg Line 1918
Havrincourt
Canal du Nord
Selle
Sambre
France and Flanders
1914–18

The Second World War 1939–45 and after

Stien 1940
Norway 1940
Mont Pincon 1944
Quarry Hill 1944
Estry
Venlo Pocket
Rhineland 1945
Reichswald
Cleve
Moyland
Hochwald
Rhine
Lingen
Uelzen
North–West Europe
1944–45

Halfaya 1941
Sidi Suleiman 1941
Tobruk 1941
Gazala 1942
Knightsbridge
Defence of Alamein
Line
Medenine 1943
Tadjera Khir
Medjez Plain
Grich el Oued
Djebel Bou Aoukaz
1943
N. Africa 1941–43
Salerno
Battipaglia

Volturno Crossing
Rocchetta e Croce
Monte Camino 1943
Anzio 1944
Campoleone
Carraceto
Trasimene Line
Advance to Florence
Monte San Michele
Catarelto Ridge
Argenta Gap
Italy 1943–45

Tumbledown Mountain
Falkland Islands 1982
Gulf 1991

The Royal Scots
(The Royal Regiment) (1st)

Tangier 1680
Namur 1695
Blenheim
Ramillies
Oudenarde
Malplaquet
Louisburg
Havannah
Egmont–op–Zee
St Lucia 1803

Corunna
Busaco
Salamanca
Vittoria
St Sebastian
Nive
Peninsula
Niagara
Waterloo
Nagpore

Maheidpoor
Ava
Alma
Inkerman
Sevastopol
Taku Forts
Peking 1860
S. Africa 1899–1902

The Great War (35 Battalions)

Mons
Le Cateau
Retreat from Mons
Marne 1914, 18
Aisne 1914
La Bassee 1914
Neuve Chapelle
Ypres 1915, 17, 18
Gravenstafel
St Julien
Frezenburg
Bellewaarde
Aubers
Festubert 1915
Loos
Somme 1916, 18
Albert 1916, 18
Bazentin
Flers–Courcelette
Le Transloy
Ancre Heights
Ancre 1916, 18
Arras 1917-18
Scarpe 1917, 18

Arleux
Pilckem
Langemarck 1917
Menin Road
Polygon Wood
Poelcappelle
Passchendaele
Cambrai 1917
St Quentin
Rosieres
Lys
Estaires
Messines 1918
Hazebrouck
Bailleul
Kemmel
Bethune
Soissonnais–Ourcq
Tardenois
Amiens
Bapaume 1918
Drocourt–Queant
Hindenburg Line
Canal du Nord

St Quentin Canal
Beaurevoir
Courtrai
Selle
Sambre
France and Flanders
   1914–18
Struma
Macedonia 1915–18
Helles
Landing at Helles
Krithia
Suvla
Scimitar Hill
Gallipoli 1915–16
Rumani
Egypt 1915–16
Gaza
El Mughar
Nebi Samwil
Jaffa
Palestine 1917–18
Archangel 1918–19

The Second World War 1939–45 and after

Dyle
Defence of Escaut
St Omer–La Bassee
Odon
Cheux
Defence of Rauray
Caen
Esquay
Mont Pincon
Aart
Nederrijn
Best
Scheldt
Flushing

Meijel
Venlo Pocket
Roer
Rhineland
Reichswald
Cleve
Goch
Rhine
Uelzen
Bremen
Artlenberg
**North–West Europe
   1940, 44–45**
Gothic Line

Marradi
Monte Gamberaldi
Italy 1944–45
South East Asia 1941
Donbaik
Kohima
Relief of Kohima
Aradura
Shwebo
Mandalay
Burma 1943–45

Gulf 1991
Wadi Al Batin

The Royal Highland Fusiliers

(Princess Margaret's Own Glasgow and Ayrshire Regiment)

(21st, 71st and 74th)

Blenheim	Vimiera	Bladensburg
Ramillies	Corunna	Waterloo
Oudenarde	Busaco	S. Africa 1851–53
Malplaquet	Fuentes d'Onor	Alma
Dettingen	Almaraz	Inkerman
Belleisle	Ciudad Rodrigo	Sevastopol
Carnatic	Badajoz	Central India
Hindoostan	Salamanca	South Africa 1879
Sholinghur	Vittoria	Tel–El–Kebir
Mysore	Pyrenees	Egypt 1882
Martinique 1794	Nivelle	Burma 1885–87
Seringapatam	Nive	Tirah
Cape of Good Hope 1806	Orthes	Modder River
Rolica	Toulouse	Relief of Ladysmith
	Peninsula	S. Africa 1899–1902

The Great War (44 Battalions)

Mons	**Arras 1917, 18**	Beaurevoir
Le Cateau	Vimy 1917	Courtrai
Retreat from Mons	Scarpe 1917, 18	Selle
Marne 1914	Arleux	Sambre
Aisne 1914	Messines 1917, 18	France and Flanders 1914–18
La Bassee 1914	Pilckem	
Ypres 1914, 15, 17, 18	Menin Road	**Doiran 1917, 18**
	Polygon Wood	Macedonia 1916–18
Langemarck 1914, 17	Passchendaele	Helles
Gheluvelt	Cambrai 1917, 18	**Gallipoli 1915–16**
Nonne Bosschen	St Quentin	Rumani
Givenchy 1914	Bapaume 1918	Egypt 1916–17
Neuve Chapelle	Rosieres	Gaza
St Julien	**Lys**	El Mughar
Aubers	Estaires	Nebi Samwill
Festubert 1915	Hazebrouck	Jerusalem
Loos	Bailleul	Jaffa
Somme 1916, 18	Kemmel	Tell'Asur
Albert 1916, 18	Bethune	**Palestine 1917–18**
Bazentin	Scherpenberg	Tigris 1916
Delville Wood	Amiens	Kut Al Amara 1917
Pozieres	Drocourt–Queant	Sharqat
Flers–Courcelette	**Hindenburg Line**	**Mesopotamia 1916–18**
Le Transloy	Havrincourt	Murmansk 1919
Ancre Heights	Canal Du Nord	**Archangel 1919**
Ancre 1916, 18	St Quentin Canal	

The Second World War 1939–45 and after

Defence of Arras
Ypres–Comines Canal
Somme 1940
Withdrawal to Seine
Withdrawal to Cherbourg
Odon
Fontenay Le Pesnil
Cheux
Defence of Rauray
Esquay
Mont Pincon
Quarry Hill
Estry
Falaise
Le Vie Crossing
La Touques Crossing
Seine 1944
Aart
Nederrijn
Best
Le Havre
Antwerp–Turnhout Canal
Scheldt
South Beveland
Walcheren Causeway

Lower Maas
Meijel
Venlo Pocket
Roer
Ourthe
Rhineland
Reichswald
Cleve
Goch
Moyland Wood
Weeze
Rhine
Ibbenburen
Dreirwalde Aller
Uelzen
Bremen
Artlenberg
N.W. Europe 1940, 44–45
Jebel Shiba
Barentu
Keran
Massawa
Abyssinia 1941
Gazala
Cauldron

Mersa Matruh
Fuka
North Africa 1940–42
Landing in Sicily
Sicily 1943
Sangro
Garigliano Crossing
Minturno
Anzio
Advance to Tiber
Italy 1943–44, 45
Madagascar
Adriatic
Middle East 1942, 44
Athens
Greece 1944–45
North Arakan
Razabil
Pinwe
Shweli
Mandalay
Burma 1944–45

Gulf 1991

The King's Own Scottish Borderers (25th)

Namur 1695
Minden
Egmont–op–Zee

Martinique 1809
Afghanistan 1878–80
Chitral

Tirah
Paardeberg
S. Africa 1900–02

The Great War (12 Battalions)

Mons
Le Cateau
Retreat from Mons
Marne 1914, 18
Aisne 1914
La Bassée 1914
Messines 1914
Ypres 1914, 15, 17, 18
Nonne Bosschen
Hill 60
Gravenstafel
St Julien
Frezenberg
Bellewaarde
Loos
Somme 1916, 18
Albert 1916, 18
Bazentin
Delville Wood

Pozieres
Guillemont
Flers–Courcelette
Morval
Le Transloy
Ancre Heights
Arras 1917, 18
Vimy 1917
Scarpe 1917, 18
Arleux
Pilckem
Langemarck 1917
Menin Road
Polygon Wood
Broodseinde
Poelcapelle
Passchendaele
Cambrai 1917, 18
St Quentin

Lys
Estaires
Hazebrouck
Kemmel
Soissonnais–Ourcq
Bapaume 1918
Drocourt–Queant
Hindenburg Line
Epehy
Canal du Nord
Courtrai
Selle
Sambre
France and Flanders
    1914–18
Italy 1917–18
Helles
Landing at Helles
Krithia

Suvla
Scimitar Hill
Gallipoli 1915–16
Rumani

Egypt 1916
Gaza
El Mughar
Nebi Samwil

Jaffa
Palestine 1917–18

The Second World War 1939–45

Dunkirk 1940
Cambes
Odon
Cheux
Defence of Rauray
Caen
Esquay
Troarn
Mont Pincon
Estry
Aart
Nederrijn
Arnhem 1944
Best
Scheldt

Flushing
Venraij
Meijel
Venlo Pocket
Roer
Rhineland
Reichswald
Cleve
Goch
Rhine
Ibbenburen
Lingen
Dreirwalde
Uelzen
Bremen

Artlenberg
North–West Europe
  1940, 44–45
North Arakan
Buthidaung
Ngakyedauk Pass
Imphal
Kanglatongbi
Ukhrul
Meiktila
Irrawaddy
Kama
Burma 1943, 45

The Korean War 1950-53 and after

Kowang–San
Maryang–San

Korea 1951–52

Gulf 1991

The Cameronians
(Scottish Rifles) (26th and 90th)

Blenheim
Ramilies
Oudenarde
Malplaquet
Mandora

Corunna
Martinique 1809
Guadaloupe 1810
S. Africa 1846–7
Sevastopol

Lucknow
Abyssinia
S. Africa 1877, 1878, 1879
Relief of Ladysmith
S. Africa 1899–1902

The Great War (27 Battalions)

Mons
Le Cateau
Retreat from Mons
Marne 1914, 18
Aisne 1914
La Bassee 1914
Armentieres 1914
Neuve Chapelle
Aubers
Loos
Somme 1916, 18
Albert 1916
Bazentin
Pozieres
Flers–Courcelette
Le Transloy

Ancre Heights
Arras 1917, 18
Scarpe 1917, 18
Arleux
Ypres 1917, 18
Pilckem
Langemarck 1917
Menin Road
Polygon Wood
Passchendaele
St Quentin
Rosieres
Avre
Lya
Hazebrouck
Bailleul

Kemmel
Scherpenberg
Soissonnais–Ourcq
Drocourt–Queant
Hindenburg Line
Epehy
Canal du Nord
St Quentin Canal
Cambrai 1918
Courtrai
Selle
Sambre
France and Flanders
  1914–18
Doiran 1917, 18
Macedonia 1915–18

Gallipoli 1915–16	Gaza	Jaffa
Rumani	El Mughar	**Palestine 1917–18**
Egypt 1916–17	Nebi Samwil	

The Second World War 1939–45

Ypres–Comines Canal	Asten	Simeto Bridgehead
Odon	Roer	**Sicily 1943**
Cheux	**Rhineland**	Garigliano Crossing
Caen	Reichswald	**Anzio**
Mont Pincon	Moyland	Advance to Tiber
Estry	**Rhine**	**Italy 1943–44**
Nederrijn	Dreirwalde	Pegu 1942
Best	Bremen	Paungde
Scheldt	Artlenburg	Yenagyaung 1942
South Beveland	**N.W. Europe 1940, 44–45**	**Chindits 1944**
Walcheron Causeway	Landing in Sicily	**Burma 1942, 44**

The Black Watch
(Royal Highland Regiment) (42nd and 73rd)

Guadaloupe 1759	**Salamanca**	**Alma**
Martinique 1762	**Pyrenees**	**Sevastopol**
Havannah	**Nivelle**	**Lucknow**
North America 1763–64	**Nive**	**Ashantee 1873–4**
Mangalore	**Orthes**	**Tel–el–Kebir**
Mysore	**Toulouse**	**Egypt 1882, 1884**
Seringapatam	**Peninsula**	**Kirbekan**
Corunna	**Waterloo**	**Nile 1884–85**
Busaco	**South Africa 1846–7**	**Paardeberg**
Fuentes d'Onor	**1851-2-3**	**S. Africa 1899–1902**

The Great War (25 Battalions)

Retreat from Mons	Thiepval	Kemmel
Marne 1914, 18	Lr Ancre Heights	Bethune
Aisne 1914	Ancre 1916	Scherpenberg
La Bassee 1914	**Arras 1917, 18**	Soissonnais–Ourcq
Ypres 1914, 17, 18	Vimy 1917	Tardenois
Langemarck 1914	Scarpe 1917, 18	Drocourt–Queant
Gheluvelt	Arleux	**Hindenburg Line**
Nonne Bosschen	Pilckem	Epehy
Givenchy 1914	Menin Road	St Quentin Canal
Neuve Chapelle	Polygon Wood	Beaurevoir
Aubers	Poelcappelle	Courtrai
Festubert	Passchendaele	Selle
Loos	Cambrai 1917, 18	Sambre
Somme 1916, 18	St Quentin	France and Flanders
Albert 1916	Bapaume 1918	1914–18
Bazentin	Rosieres	**Doiran 1917**
Delville Wood	**Lys**	Macedonia 1915–18
Pozieres	Estares	Egypt 1916
Flers–Courcelette	Messines 1918	Gaza
Morval	Hazebrouck	Jerusalem

Tell'Asur	Damascus	**Kut al Amara 1917**
Megiddo	Palestine 1917–18	Baghdad
Sharon	Tigris 1916	Mesopotamia 1915–17

The Second World War 1939–45

Defence of Arras	**Rhine**	Sferro
Ypres–Comines Canal	North West Europe	Gerbini
Dunkirk 1940	1940-44-45	Adrano
Somme 1940	Barkasan	Sferro Hills
St Valery–en–Caux	British Somaliland 1940	**Sicily 1943**
Saar	**Tobruk 1941**	**Cassino II**
Breville	Tobruk Sortie	Liri Valley
Odon	**El Alamein**	Advance to Florence
Fontenay le Pesnil	Advance on Tripoli	Monte Scalari
Defence of Rauray	Medenine	Casa Fortis
Caen	Zemlet el Lebene	Rimini Line
Falaise	Mareth	Casa Fabbri Ridge
Falaise Road	**Akarit**	Savio Bridgehead
Le Vie Crossing	Wadi Akarit East	Italy 1944–45
Le Havre	Djebel Roumana	Athens
Lower Maas	Medjez Plain	Greece 1944–45
Venlo Pocket	Si Mediene	**Crete**
Ourthe	**Tunis**	Heraklion
Rhineland	North Africa 1941–43	Middle East 1941
Reischwald	Landing in Sicily	Chindits 1944
Goch	Vizzini	**Burma 1944**

The KoreanWar 1950-53

The Hook 1952	Korea 1951–52

The Highlanders
(Seaforth, Gordons and Camerons) (72nd, 75th, 78th, 79th and 92nd)

Carnatic	**Vittoria**	**Charasiah**
Hindoostan	**Nivelle**	**Kabul 1879**
Mysore	**Nive**	**Kandahar 1880**
Seringapatam	**Orthes**	**Afghanistan 1878–80**
Egmont–op–Zee	**Toulouse**	**Tel–El–Kebir**
Mandora	**Peninsula**	**Egypt 1882–84**
Cape of Good Hope	**Waterloo**	**Nile 1884–85**
1806	**South Africa 1835**	**Chitral**
Maida	**Alma**	**Tirah**
Corunna	**Sevastopol**	**Atbara**
Busaco	**Koosh–ab**	**Khartoum**
Fuentes d'Onor	**Persia**	**Defence of Ladysmith**
Java	**Deihl 1857**	**Paardeberg**
Alamaraz	**Lucknow**	**S. Africa 1899–1902**
Salamanca	**Central India**	**Gulf 1991**
Pyreenes	**Peiwar Kotal**	

The Great War (32 Battalions)

Mons
Le Cateau
Retreat from Mons
Marne 1914, 18
Aisne 1914
La Bassee 1914
Armentieres 1914
Messines 1914
Ypres 1914, 15, 17, 18
Langemarck 1914
Gheluvelt
Nonne Bosschen
Festubert 1914, 15
Givenchy 1914
Neuve Chapelle
Hill 60
Gravenstafel
St Julien
Frezenberg
Bellewaarde
Aubers
Hooge 1915
Loos
Somme 1916, 18
Albert 1916, 18
Bazentin
Delville Wood

Pozieres
Guillemont
Flers–Courcelette
Moval
Le Transloy
Ancre Heights
Ancre 1916
Arras 1917, 18
Vimy 1917
Scarpe 1917, 18
Arleux
Bullecourt
Pilckem
Menin Road
Polygon Wood
Broodseinde
Poelcappelle
Passchendaele
Cambrai 1917, 18
St Quentin
Bapaume 1918
Rosieres
Lys
Estaires
Messines 1918
Hazebrouck
Bailleul

Kemmel
Bethune
Soissonais–Ourcq
Tardenois
Droccourt–Queant
Hindenburg Line
Epehy
Canal du Nord
St Quentin Canal
Courtrai
Selle
Valenciennes
Sambre
France and Flanders
    1914–18
Piave
Vittorio Veneto
Italy 1917–18
Struma
Macedonia 1915–18
Megiddo
Sharon
Palestine
Tigris 1916
Kut al Amara 1917
Baghdad
Mesopotamia 1915–18

The Second World War 1939–45

Defence of Escaut
St Omer–La Bassee
Ypres–Comines Canal
Dunkirk 1940
Somme 1940
Withdrawal to Seine
St Valery–en–Caux
Odon
Cheux
Caen
Troarn
Mont Pincon
Quarry Hill
Falaise
Falaise Road
Dives Crossing
La Vie Crossing
Lisieux
Nederrijn
Best
Le Havre
Lower Maas
Meijel

Venlo Pocket
Ourthe
Rhineland
Reichswald
Cleve
Goch
Moyland
Rhine
Uelzen
Artlenberg
North West Europe
    1940, 44–45
Agordat
Keren
Abyssinia 1941
Sidi Barrani
Tobruk 1941, 42
Gubi II
Carmusa
Gazala
El Alamein
Advance on Tripoli
Mareth

Wadi Zigzaou
Akarit
Djebel Roumana
Medjez Plain
North Africa 1940–43
Landing in Sicily
Augusta
Francofonte
Sferro
ehp2. Adrano
Sferro Hills
Sicily 1943
Garigliano Crossing
Anzio
Cassino I
Poggio del Grillo
Gothic Line
Tavoleto
Coriano
Pian di Castello
Rimini Line
San Marino
Monte Reggiano

Italy 1943–45
Madagascar
Middle East 1942
Imphal
Shenam Pass
Litan

Kohima
Relief of Kohima
Naga Village
Aradura
Tengnoupal
Shwebo

Mandalay
Ava
Irrawaddy
Mt Popa
Burma 1942–45

The Argyll and Sutherland Highlanders
(Princess Louise's) (91st and 93rd)

Cape of Good Hope 1806
Rolica
Vimiera
Corunna
Pyrenees
Nivelle
Nive

Orthes
Toulouse
Peninsula
S. Africa 1846–7, 1851-2-3
Alma
Balaklava
Sevastopol

Lucknow
South Africa 1879
Modder River
Paardeberg
S. Africa 1899–1902

The Great War (27 Battalions)

Mons
Le Cateau
Retreat from Mons
Marne 1914, 18
Aisne 1914
La Bassee 1914
Messines 1914, 18
Armentieres 1914
Ypres 1915, 17, 18
Gravenstafel
St Julien
Frezenberg
Bellewaardie
Festubert 1915
Loos
Somme 1916, 18
Albert 1916, 18
Bazentin
Delville Wood
Pozieres
Flers-Courcelette
Morval
Le Transloy

Ancre Heights
Ancre 1916
Arras 1917, 18
Scarpe 1917,18
Arleux
Pilckem
Menin Road
Polygon Wood
Broodseinde
Poelcappelle
Passchendaele
Cambrai 1917, 18
St Quentin
Bapaume 1918
Rosieres
Lys
Estaires
Hazebrouck
Bailleul
Kemmel
Bethune
Soissonnais–Ourcq
Tardenois Amiens

Hindenburg Line
Epehy
Canal du Nord
St Quentin Canal
Beaurevoir
Courtrai
Selle
Sambre
France and Flanders
    1914–18
Italy 1917, 18
Struma
Doiran 1917 18
Macedonia 1915–18
Gallipoli 1915–18
Rumani
Egypt 1916
Gaza
El Mughar
Nebi Samwil
Jaffa
Palestine 1917–18

The Second World War 1939–45

Somme 1940
Odon
Trourmauville Bridge
Caen
Esquay
Mont Pincon
Quarry Hill
Estry
Falaise
Dives Crossing

Aart
Lower Maas
Meijel
Venlo Pocket
Ourthe
Rhineland
Reichswald
Rhine
Uelzen
Artlenberg

N.W. Europe 1940, 44–45
Abyssinia 1941
Sidi Barrani
El Alamein
Medenine
Akarit
Djebel Azzag 1942
Kef Ouiba Pass
Mine de Sedjenane
Medjez Plain

Longstop Hill 1943
North Africa 1940–43
Landing in Sicily
Gerbini
Adrano
Centuripe
Sicily 1943
Termoli
Sangro
Cassino II

Liri Valley
Aquino
Monte Casalino
Monte Spaduro
Monte Grande
Senio
Santerno Crossing
Argenta Gap
Italy 1943–45
Crete

Heraklion
Middle East 1941
North Malaya
Grik Road
Central Malaya
Ipoh
Slim River
Singapore Island
Malaya 1941–42

The Korean War 1950–53

Pakchon

Korea 1950–51

Appendix 2

The Territorial Army

The Territorial Army, with its volunteer part-time soldiers, is a popular and widely accepted part of Scottish life. Better known simply as the TA, the origins of the Territorials date back to the Rifle Volunteers raised in the 1850s. These units were raised locally and, consequently, had strong local and often trade, or professional attachments. Originally they were not subject to military law and were, in essence, local uniformed rifle clubs under the direction of the Lords Lieutenant of counties. They were clearly distinguishable from the Militia who were conscripted largely by ballot and from the Fencibles, both of which were raised during the French Wars in the 1790s for home defence. It is an interesting quirk of history that the Militia always considered themselves superior to the Volunteers.

In 1877, the Volunteers became subject to military control and in 1881, they were linked for the first time with regimental districts and parent regular regiments, while the Militia formally became the reserve of the regular army. Major reforms in 1908, under Lord Haldane, resulted in the Volunteers officially becoming Territorial Battalions with a reserve field force role. A formal numbering system was also adopted: for most regiments, the 1st and 2nd battalions were regular army battalions, the 3rd Battalion was the Reserve (Militia) Battalion while the 4th and subsequent battalions were the Territorial Battalions.

These Territorial Battalions went on to acquit themselves with great distinction during the First and Second World Wars. They fought in formations of Territorial Divisions, which in their turn acquired formidable reputations; the 51st Highland and the 52nd Lowland Divisions are names which have acquired a special place in Scottish military history. Not only were the divisional names and numbers famous; individual Territorial units also attracted particular renown including the London Scottish, the Liverpool Scottish, the Tyneside Scottish, the Lovat Scouts, the 'Dandy' 9th Battalion of the Royal Scots, the 7th Argylls, the 4/5th Black Watch and the Glasgow Highlanders.

Major reductions of the TA followed the Army re-organisations of 1967 and further adjustments are being made in the 1990s, when some of the famous names will disappear from the Army list. However, the concept of the volunteer remains the same. Officers and service men and women all volunteer to join. They are paid to train on a regular evening and weekend basis with a committment to attend an annual camp for two weeks each year, together with a generous tax-free bounty payment for attendance and for achieving set standards of fitness, skill at arms, first aid, nuclear and biological warfare, etc. The officers and soldiers are there because they want to be there, bringing to the service an unparalleled range of civilian skills and enthusiasm.

Appendix 3

Scottish Military Music

Music has always been an important element in the day-to-day life, ceremony and style of the Scottish regiments. Over the years various instruments in different combinations have been in use in these regiments: fifes, drums, bugles, string, brass and wind instruments, and of course, bagpipes. Fifes, drums, bugles, and pipes were all used to convey signals in the field until the development of field radio communications and they are still in use today to mark the timings and the main events of the day in barracks. The 'Band of Music', or Military Band, which was developed initially for the private entertainment of the officers, evolved throughout the 18th and 19th centuries as new instruments were invented and introduced. In 1994, Military Bands in individual Scottish line regiments were abolished and replaced by The Highland Band and The Lowland Band.

Nearly all the Scottish regiments seem to have had fifes and drums during their history, but these gradually fell from fashion in the second half of the 19th century and while the Scottish regiments commonly had pipers in their ranks, the allocation of a Pipe Major and five pipers per regiment was not officially recognised until 1854 and then only for the Highland regiments. The pipers played the ancient classical pipe music (*Piobaireachd*), the lighter music of strathspeys, reels and popular airs and later, the more formal pipe marches. There is evidence that pipers played together, but did not play with the drummers; pipe bands comprising pipers and bass, tenor and side-drummers were a later 19th century development.

The Scottish regiments can justifiably lay claim to having played a major part in the preservation, adaptation and development of pipe music as we know it today, with some of the greatest composers and performers of our time having been serving soldiers. Other developments have been the introduction of 'seconds', or harmony, in pipe music and the Pipe and the Military Bands playing together.

Today, the music of the Scottish regiments is played by the members of the Pipe Band, under the direction of the Pipe Major. The pipers and drummers are of course serving soldiers as well as highly qualified musicians and are drawn from the rifle companies. Select pipers are trained at the world famous Army School of Piping at Edinburgh Castle for the coveted Pipe Major's certificate.

As for the music itself, there are specific and standardised drum beatings and bugle calls for particular occasions and set tunes for regimental marches, slow marches, etc., for both the Pipe Band and the Military Band. The traditional and highly stylised set pieces are played at dinner nights, formal parades, tattoos and beatings of retreat. Dancing has also always formed part of this musical tradition, especially in the Highland regiments where men still dance in the old way, which in the civilian world is now primarily a preserve of young women.

Appendix 4
Scottish Units In Other Countries

Not really enough is known or has been recorded about the many Scots, men and women, and units with Scottish origins who have served the world over. Our national pride, martial skills and tendency to band together, particularly when far from home, has resulted in the emergence of some formidable military leaders and a number of large and small military units with Scottish associations and traditions. Many of these units are obscure, unappreciated and under-researched. Many have long since been disbanded, while some have survived amalgamations, changes of designation and the complete reorder of the world security situation.

In some cases there has, in recent years, been a renewal of interest often based upon the ever increasing popularity of pipe bands, classical pipe music and the desire of individuals to search for, and proclaim with pride, their national and ethnic origins. Nowhere is the interest greater than in the USA and in Canada.

The United States and Canada

A number of British regiments, particularly Highland regiments, now disbanded, are known to have served in North America against the French. One of these was the 77th Regiment (Montgomery's Highlanders) raised at Stirling in 1757 and disbanded in 1763. They sailed to Halifax, saw service against the French and were later quartered in New York. The 78th Regiment (Fraser's Highlanders) also saw service in Canada and Nova Scotia between 1757 and 1763. When the French war ended in 1763, the officers and men of both of these regiments, numbering some 2,500 men, were given the chance of either settling in America or returning home. Those who elected to remain in America were given a grant of land and it was primarily from these men that the 84th Regiment (Royal Highland Emigrants) was raised in 1775 at the beginning of the American War of Independence.

Under Lt. Col. Allan MacLean, two battalions of Highland Emmigrants of ten companies each mustered at Lake Champlain. By 1778 each battalion numbered 1,000 men and included former soldiers and Highland settlers, many from Nova Scotia. This was indeed an unusual regiment, having been raised on nationalistic lines in North America. They played their part in foiling American designs on Canada but 1783 the 84th was reduced and given grants of land, 1st Battalion men settling mainly in Canada while 2nd Battalion men went primarily to Nova Scotia. Those who were already North American settlers remained but many others returned home.

Others less well documented British Highland regiments were raised in Scotland at this time for service in North America. The 71st Regiment (Fraser's Highlanders) was raised at Stirling by the same Simon Fraser, now a Major General, who had raised the 78th Regiment in 1757. The new regiment, the 71st, numbered 2,340 men. On the voyage to North America, one of the transport ships sailed into Boston harbour and, having failed to appreciate that the town had been evacuated by the British, was immediately captured by the Americans. After distinguished service in the American war, Fraser's troops were among those who surrendered at Yorktown.

The 74th (The Argyll Highlanders) under Col. John Campbell of Barbeck, raised in 1778, disbanded 1783, and the 76th (MacDonald's Highlanders) under Lord MacDonald of Sleat, raised 1777, disbanded 1784, also served in America. Macdonald's Highlanders were amongst the force which surrendered at Yorktown in 1781 and remained prisoners in Virginia until 1783 when the survivors embarked for home at New York and were subsequently disbanded at Stirling Castle.

Both as individuals and in groups, many Scots fought on both sides in the American war. Highlanders in the main were loyal to the Crown, being driven not so much by their loyalty to George III but by their disdain for the Lowlanders and Ulstermen who were prominent in the rebel cause. Notable individuals included the 80-year-old Donald Mc Donald; Allan MacDonald who was captured at Moores Creek Bridge in 1776 and his wife Flora McDonald who had helped the Young Pretender escape following the disaster at Culloden thirty years earlier; and Donald MacCrimmon, the last of the MacCrimmon family to act as hereditary pipers to the Macleods of Skye. MacCrimmon served in the Caledonian Volunteers, later Cathcart's Legion, and in Tarleton's Legion.

Today Scottish clan and family names can be found in all ranks of the US services. At least one American serviceman, Sgt J.T. Scott 163rd (US) General Hospital, attended piping courses under Pipe Major William Ross at Edinburgh Castle during the Second World War, and in 1950 the US Sixth Army formed its own pipe band. Numerous American serviceman have served in Scotland, particularly in the US Air Force and submarine bases and Scots and Americans now work together as part of NATO's Implementation Force in Bosnia.

After American independence, the defence of Canada became a real concern. Service in the Canadian militia was compulsory and the Scots of Stormont, Dundas and Glengarry Counties played a notable part in the defence of their emerging nation.

The Glengarry Light Infantry Fencible Regiment (1812–1816) and the First and Second Regiments of Glengarry Militia (1812–1815), the First Regiment of Dundas Militia and the First Regiment of Stormont Militia, all saw service in the War of 1812 against the Americans. A number of regiments, primarily manned by Scots emigrants, were raised during the tension of the 1830s but the majority of Canadian Scottish regiments find their origins in the 1860s, coinciding with the Volunteer movement in the United Kingdom. Many of these were, and still are closely affiliated to Scottish regiments, wearing their tartan and carrying on their Scottish traditions.

These Canadian Scottish regiments acquitted themselves with great distinction in the South African War, the First World War, the Second World War and the Korean War. Today they continue this traditions, having earned a remarkable reputation as effective and respected 'peacekeepers' with the United Nations and NATO.

Up until the 1860s Scottish regiments which formed part of the garrison of Canada included the 79th Cameron Highlanders, the 93rd Sutherland Highlanders, the 42nd Royal Highland Regiment and the 78th Highlanders (Ross-shire Buffs, the Duke of Albany's). Not only did these regiments contribute to the development of Canadian society and culture, they also contributed to the emigrant population, many men taking their discharge in Canada to begin a new life.

The role of Canadian Scottish Regiments is lengthy and distinguished and includes The Black Watch (Royal Highlander Regiment) of Canada, The Perth Regiment, The Highland Light Infantry of Canada, The Lorne Scots (Peel, Dufferin and Halton Regiment), The Stormont, Glengarry and Dundas Highlanders, The New Brunswick Scottish, The Pictou Highlanders, The North Nova Scotia Highlanders, The Cape Breton Highlanders, The Cameron Highlanders of Ottowa The Essex Scottish, The 48th Highlanders of Canada, The Argyll & Sutherland Highlanders of Canada (Princess Louise's), The Lake Superior Scottish

Regiment, The Queen's Own Cameron Highlanders of Canada, The Calgary Highlanders, The Seaforth Highlanders of Canada, The Canadian Scottish Regiment (Princess Mary's), and The Toronto Scottish Regiment. There were in addition a number of anti-tank and anti-aircraft regiments with Scottish associations as well as the 13th Scottish Light Dragoons, who were disbanded in 1936.

There have been a number of Canadian Scottish recipients of the Victoria Cross amongst the most celebrated of these was the award to Piper James Cleland Richardson. Richardson was born in Lanarkshire and before the First World War his family moved to Canada where his father, David Richardson, became Chief of Police in British Columbia. In August 1914 he joined the 72nd Seaforth Highlanders of Canada (16th Battalion (Canadian) Scottish). In October 1916, Piper

Piper James Cleland Richardson

Richardson was serving as part of the 1st Canadian Division who were to advance on a formidable fortified position known as ' The Quadrilateral' and Regina Trench on the Somme Battlefield, northwest of the village of Earcourt. The Canadian attack ground to a standstill in the face of wire defences and they could advance no further. Piper Richardson struck up his pipes and for a good ten minutes walked up and down in front of the wire playing. His citation reads, 'The effect was instantaneous. Inspired by his splendid example the company rushed the wire with such fury and determination that the obstacle was overcome and the position captured'.

Later in the same action Piper Richardson was killed retrieving his pipes from the battlefield. He is buried in Adanac Military Cemetery.

South Africa

South Africa, so recently and so happily returned to the Commonwealth of Nations, also has many links with Scotland and a long history of Scottish regimental affiliations. The oldest of these, The First City, lays claim to origins in the Grahamstown Volunteers, dating from before 1835 with Scottish associations dating from 1875.

South African Scottish regiments also include The Capetown Highlanders, raised in 1885, and whose affiliated regiment is The Highlanders. The Capetown Highlanders are based in the beautiful old castle at Cape Town. During the First World War many of their men served inthe 4th South African Infantry (South African Scottish) and in 1943 they were combined with First city and entitled First City/Capetown Highlanders. In 1947 The Queen Mother became their colonel- in-chief and in the following year, they were given their present title.

Their battle honours include 'Bechuanaland 1897', 'South Africa 1899-1902' and 'South-West Africa 1915'. In 1947 when Queen Elizabeth II celebrated her 21st birthday in Cape Town, the Cape Town Scottish provided the guard of honour. When Her Majesty made her historic visit to Cape Town in March 1995 the Cape Town Highlanders claimed their place once more and,

Officer, Transvaal Scottish

headed by their pipes and drums, formed the guard for Her Majesty at Woltemade Commonwealth Cemetery.

Other South African Scottish units include the Witwatersand Rifles, raised in1899 and the 1st Anti-Tank Regiment, South African Artillery (Pretoria Highlanders). In 1939, the Witwatersand Rifles wore the uniform of The Cameronians (Scottish Rifles) while the Pretoria Highlanders wore Hunting Stewart tartan.

The Transvaal Scottish, with their outstanding Headquarters Mess and Museum in one of the oldest houses in Johannesburg, is another regiment with strong links with Scotland. This distinguished regiment was raised as the Transvaal Scottish Volunteers on 9th June 1902 and in a proud career of service which has included German South-West Africa in 1914–1915, Tobruk and Alamein, the regiment has won 18 battle honours. Their tartan is Murray of Atholl, while the pipers wear Murray of Tullibardine. The Regimental March is 'The Atholl Highlanders'.

New Zealand and Australia
New Zealand and Australia have always had a very strong connections with Scotland and large number of Scots have fought with distinction in the service of these countries. Although disbanded in the 1880s, four Scottish Volunteer companies were formed in New Zealand: the Christchurch Highlanders, Dunedin Highland Rifles, Wanganui Highland Rifles and Wellington Highland Rifles. The New Zealand Scottish Regiment was raised in 1939 as the result of the enthusiasm of local Scottish societies; only those men who could prove Scottish descent were accepted and the regiment became affiliated to The Black Watch. To their great disappointment they were not sent on active service as a regiment and in 1943 they were drafted. In 1949 the unit was reformed and entitled 1st Armoured Car Regiment (New Zealnd Scottish) Royal New Zealand Amoured Corps. A number of battatlions of the Royal New Zealand Infantry Regiment are still proudly affiliated with Scottish regiments and maintain close ties with them.

Of the many New Zealanders who have won the Victoria cross at least one was of Scottish origin. Lance Corporal, later Captain, Samual Frickleton was born in Clackmannan in Stirlingshire on 1st April 1891. While serving with the 3rd Battalion, the 3rd New Zealand (Rifle) Brigade, New Zealand Expeditionary Force, he won his award at Messines on 7th June 1917. Samual Frickleton died in Wellington, New Zealnd on 1st September 1971.

The history of Australian Scottish regiments included the 5th Battalion (The Victorian Scottish regiment) raised in 1898; the 16th Battalion (The Cameron Highlanders of Western Australia) raised in 1899; the 27th Battalion (The South Australian Scottish Regiment) raised in 1912; the 30th Battalion (The New South Wales Scottish Regiment) raised in 1885 and the 41st Battalion (The Byron Regiment). With the exception of the 41st Battalion all of these regiments sent contingents to the South African War between 1899–1902. Therafter they all won extensive battle honours in the First World War, including 'Somme 1916', 'Ypres 1917', 'Passchendaele', 'Anzac', 'Suvla' and 'Gallipoli 1915'. The fighting reputation of Australian forces was hard won and well deserved. That reputation was re-enforced in New Guinea, the Western Desert, Korea, Malaya, Borneo and Vietnam. In total 96 Australians have won the Victoria Cross. The last four were won in Vietnam and they were the last Australian Victoria Crosses before the Australian Government established an Australian national honours system in 1975. In 1989, following a request from the Australian Government, Her Majesty The Queen agreed to the restoration of the V.C. as Australia's highest decoration for courage in battle.

The Scottish connection remains strong in the Australian armed forces. Scottish names run through the ranks of all services at all levels and the visitor could imagine themselves not far from Princes Street in Edinburgh when the Pipes and Drums and Australian Scots march past in Sydney on ANZAC Day.

Author's Note
One of the great pleasures of being an historian is that of recording the achievements of those who have gone before and an ensuring that justice is done to their endeavours. It has proved very difficult to build up an accurate and up-to-date picture of Scots and Scottish units overseas. Consequently, there will undoubtedly be omissions in the preceding text and perhaps some errors. For these I apologise, and I would welcome all correspondence on this topic (addressed to me at The Scots at War Trust, e-mail IASH@ed.ac.uk,) in the hope that I shall be able to correct any faults in the third edition.